Throat Punch Lessons

Douglas Armendarez

Acknowledgments

A special thanks to my terrific wife, Heather, who spent hours and hours trying to fix my seemingly unfixable diction. I would be remiss not to also thank my daughter Anabelle for forcing me to stop working and go outside to play some tennis now and again, and for Meridian Hill for hanging out with her when I was busy.

To my son Carter, who inspired the focus of this book, thank you for motivating me to continue to do what needs to be done even when I feel too tired to push on.

Thanks also to Britt Ashcraft for designing a compelling cover, and Ryan Dunn for creating a blurb that pulls the focus of the book together.

Throughout the process of writing this book, many have helped provide data, interview content, and insights. The book would not have happened without your help. Gary Goltz, your sacrifice of time and your willingness to share your experience was vital. Thanks to Richard Andrew Watson for answering my questions, even when it was uncomfortable. In addition, thank you Dave Guerrero for giving me the time you could, and Amber Horn and Germaine Soriano for recounting some old memories.

A special thanks to Danya Quintero, Jocelyn, and Blanca Nieves Chavez-Quintero for all of your stories, help with translation and insights into the life of Everilda Watson. And, many thanks to Louisa Jaslow, and the camera crew, for the generous support and guidance throughout the *I.D. Discovery Channel* interview.

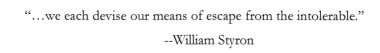

"…we each devise our means of escape from the intolerable."

--William Styron

Daybook Journal: 6/18/2014

I've taught senior English for most of my career, so I've seen hundreds of my students graduate. It's always exciting to see their sense of accomplishment and all of the hoopla that comes with the graduation ceremony. Finally my own son graduated, and I thought I would cry the entire time, like a giant baby, and that I'd have to hide my tears, but when the day came I found the ceremony long, boring and uncomfortable. My back began to seize up just like it would at any long ceremony. Our son has been with us for nearly our entire marriage, so the idea of him going off to college seems almost wrong. My wife has been going through the cycles of grief—she has even considered moving back East to live near him.

When my son was in junior high, I remember helping students write their college entrance application essays, and most of them came from disadvantage. Plenty of them have had real struggle: foster homes, parent issues, no money, and no support. I wondered, what is my white middle class son going to have to write about? We're going to have to spin some hardship for him when it comes time to write his college application essay.

I'd like to think the stories in *Throat Punch Lessons* stand alone, that the reader would take their own meaning from them, but my wife told me I needed some sort of introduction. She's usually right about most things. The thing about getting punched in the throat is you generally don't see it coming. If you did see it coming you wouldn't stand there and allow a fist to crush your Adam's apple. You would work to avoid the panic and momentary inability to breathe that directly follows a solid throat punch. Sometimes that pain and panic fade away, yet some of the unlucky few are left with a crushed wind pipe, and some of those never catch their breath and lie in the street and die. Is there a lesson learned? I guess that depends on your perspective and whether you're still alive or not. Some would say there is a lesson in all struggle and we learn and become sharpened. Yet, it seems that there are times a throat punch leaves behind no real lesson, rather it steals something from you, something that can never be replaced or regained.

It has always struck me that some teachers believe their lessons are vital and necessary, and they are irreplaceable. I've always seen that I'm the one learning most of the lessons. It's been my pleasure to be witness as a kid improves an essay, or is excited about a book or a newly acquired philosophy, or makes sense of one of many obstacles faced and overcome. I hope these stories work to celebrate people, lives cut short, and experiences hindered, yet celebrated and given meaning.

Near the end of junior high our son was diagnosed with an extreme form of narcolepsy. In short, some of his brain cells were permanently destroyed, which help us regulate sleep we need at night. Now his body struggles to make up that lost sleep during the rest of the day. It was a punch to the throat that came out of nowhere. All of a sudden he was stricken with a disability that would affect him for the rest of his life. This energetic boy, which once was full of life and the hardest worker on his sports teams and in his classes, now struggled to stay awake as he went through his day. He will never be able to stay up late to study, probably never drive a car, and never be able to train as hard as others at his given sport. I try to avoid thinking about the boy he once was, because it makes me sad; it makes me angry. But, also I'm so proud of what he has overcome to become who he is now. We don't treat him like he's disabled; he doesn't act like he's disabled. He's lucky. His windpipe is permanently damaged, but he's walking and breathing. He finally has something to write about in his college application essay.

1

Application Essay

Carter Armendarez

Wesleyan University: Class of 2018

I fell asleep in class again despite trying my hardest to concentrate on the lecture. My first ever detention was given to me for what my teacher called being "lazy." I have been struggling to stay awake since middle school. Several doctors' appointments and sleep studies later I was diagnosed with narcolepsy. In high school, my narcolepsy continued to worsen. Walking to class and laughing with friends became harder for reasons unknown to me at the time. So, after more trips to the neurologist, I was diagnosed with cataplexy, a condition where extreme emotions like laughter or anger weaken muscles. My cataplexy was so extreme my joints would momentarily weaken to where I could not stand. This was a problem because wrestling season was coming up. I was heartbroken that I might not be able to continue playing the sport I had been trying to master my entire life. I was rescued by a new drug called Xyrem which allowed me to continue wrestling and going to high school as a normal student. Due to narcolepsy and Xyrem I have to go to sleep early and carefully plan my life to avoid constant daytime sleepiness.

Xyrem did change my life but was far from a miracle drug. Side effects of Xyrem include extreme anxiety, which I began to struggle with soon after taking it. Following my sophomore year I transferred to a school where I didn't know anyone, considerably increasing my anxiety. Connecting with people became difficult and I became uncomfortable in social settings. Sweating profusely in public was a fear as I had panic attacks that left me sweating in routine social settings that had not bothered me before I started Xyrem. Again came the cycle of going to see doctors so I could function as a normal person. None of the doctors were any help. Some doctors didn't believe or understand how severe my anxiety was, just like the doctors from a few years prior that thought I was just lazy and didn't really have narcolepsy. Through my own research, I learned many people that suffer with narcolepsy also have extreme anxiety. This is due to low levels of Serotonin, a chemical that controls impulsivity in the body. The body creates Serotonin during sleep which is why narcoleptics usually have a limited supply. I was prescribed Serotonin medication and was able to calm down and make friends on the wrestling team. I am now the captain.

My narcolepsy has shaped my work ethic. To achieve success in academics and athletics, I have had to learn to manage my time, as I am not able to stay up late at night studying like my friends. Narcolepsy has been a huge obstacle to my performance, but I have overcome this weakness and excelled in my sport and in the classroom. For example, I was able to qualify for state in wrestling, and place top 12 in the California State Wrestling Championships in a state with over 1900 wrestling programs. I won the Riverside County Championships, was MVP of the League Championships, and was a CIF Sectional Champion. I accomplished these things in spite of not being able to sleep enough to get all the REM sleep a normal person needs. Instead I took a nap between matches, often waking up and immediately wrestling. In spite of being forced to take my medication and going to sleep shortly after sunset I have managed to maintain near a 4.0 GPA. The only time my grades have dropped below that was my 10th grade year when we struggled getting my medication and diagnosis on target. My struggles with narcolepsy and anxiety have made me realize any task can be conquered with perseverance and planning. In the future I know there will be no obstacle too challenging I won't be able to accomplish.

Daybook Journal: 7/20/2009

Our son is a great wrestler. He just won the Winter National Judo Championships for the second year in a row. He has only done judo for about two months. The kid in the finals looked pretty well versed in the sport of judo, yet he seemed too unfamiliar with wrestling attacks to defend his positioning. I think the referees were a little irritated with a wrestling kid coming in and winning the tournament.

Judo means "gentle way" which makes it sound nice and inviting, yet it can be anything but that. I saw one of the bigger competitors get his arm caught in his uniform, and his arm bent entirely in the wrong direction. He fell directly face first into the mat and did not move. A group of men surrounded him and shielded the crowd by holding up some sort of white sheet. People continued to walk by the mat slowing down to take a peak around the sheets and take a look at the grotesquely twisted and bent appendage. I was grateful our son got through the tournament with no injuries.

Daybook Journal: 10/5/2001

What is truth? That was the question last night in the class I teach on critical thinking. It's a night class, so you get a wide range of students, some old, some young, some interested, and some just trying to get through this last course so they can transfer to a four year college. But, who doesn't want to know what truth is? Most are interested in truth.

We talked about Ishmael, in Melville's *Moby Dick*, a parallel many writers have used to explore the concept of perspective. Perspectivism is the theory that there are as many truths as there are perspectives. The whale, who arguably could be viewing two distinctly different objective sets of data, being that their eyes are on opposite sides of their heads making it impossible to see one reality with both eyes at the same time, serves as a good example for the idea that in the same moment of time the whale might experience multiple truths. I drew a horribly scaled picture of a group of kids on the shoreline, eating popsicles, waving vigorously at the whale as it peeked its head up above the water for a breath. Like most young kids on buses they hoped vigorous waving might elicit some reaction from the whale. On the other side of the whale, on the opposite side of the board, I drew a stick figure in a small boat getting ready to throw a harpoon at the whale. In the thoughts of Ishmael, "...both his eyes, in themselves, must simultaneously act; but is his brain so much more comprehensive, combining, and subtle than man's, that he can at the same moment of time attentively examine two distinct prospects, one on one side of him, and the other in an exactly opposite direction?" Then, I asked the class to explain the truth of the whale in this experience.

Science has explored the whale's eye and the relationship between what it sees, how it sees, and what type of consciousness results within the whale's mind. Nobody can say for sure.

Yet, this is one whale, and maybe it can make sense of what it sees, and maybe it does formulate a single subjective opinion, but we are all separate people, none of us generally seeing the same thing, even when we are in the same shared moment. We all come to an experience with our own backgrounds. Spinoza, the 17th century Dutch philosopher, made the point that if you asked a group of triangles what God looked like, they would all give God attributes of a triangle. Students agreed with the idea and surmised God probably looked a lot like we do.

The idea here is there is no one objective truth, but rather there are only subjective truths, and the more we can collect the closer to a truth we might come. Contradiction will exist, yet there will be a thread that reveals more truth.

*

What follows are a collection of interviews and recollections concerning the Everilda Watson murder (note: "Eve" was used as the spelling of Everilda, because that's how some of her family spelled it, and that's how John Watson spelled her name in his letters, rather than the "Evie" spelling used in court documents). The pieces in this chapter purposely omit the names of most of the players involved so that the reader might focus on the collective truths and perspectives rather than focus on the witnesses themselves. The strategy of the chapter follows what has been referred to as the Roshomon Effect, or the technique of presenting several perspectives of an incident retold by several different individuals. "Roshomon" is originally a short story written by the Japanese writer Ryunosuke Akutagawa, which uses the technique of retelling its story of a murdered samurai as retold by several individuals. In the end we find there is no one answer, no one objective truth.

Ideas and interviews have been modified and arranged to fit the purposes of the chapter. Yet, the content and force behind the data has remained. Likewise, the John Watson letters have been taken and rewritten in the voice and tone of John Watson, while working to maintain accuracy of content. The decision was made not to enter the word for word writing of John Watson, but rather to capture his voice and thought patterns.

2

In a Desert

Ex-math teacher, John Watson, was arrested and convicted for murdering his wife, Everilda Watson, on their Las Vegas vacation. Everilda Watson was last seen in Las Vegas, during a trip to celebrate her 50th birthday, on July 13th, 2006. John Watson claimed the two separated earlier that day, to split up and go play their games of choice, yet Everilda failed to return to their meeting spot at their scheduled time, 3 a.m.

The police believe Watson killed his wife after bringing her to the Tuscany Suites Hotel, where he dismantled her corpse with an electric saw and a box cutter. He was recorded, by surveillance video, as buying an electric band saw, an extension cord, Clorox bleach, antifreeze, a 40-count box of plastic bags, incense, and odor neutralizer.

She is said to have vanished. Reports state, "He [John Watson] was carrying a wig, several thousand dollars, a fake ID and a ticket for a bus that was about to leave for El Paso, Texas." He was arrested three weeks after his wife was reported missing, and they arrested him at a diner, adjacent to the Greyhound bus depot in Claremont, CA only an hour before his bus was scheduled to depart.

Everilda's body has not been found. Her blood showed up on a bloody tarp found in Nevada, and blood spatter and human tissue were later found in their Jeep Cherokee, spotted parked outside John Watson's Las Vegas hotel. Watson maintained his wife had cut her finger in the car opening a package of flashlights, and some of the blood did not get cleaned up properly. Investigators also found Everilda's blood in the shower drain, and two blood stains in the carpet of their hotel room. Later police would find Everilda's blood and DNA on the barrel of a revolver, as well as the 13 remaining trash bags, and the box cutter, both with his wife's blood on them. Furthermore, it was reported upon his arrest that John Watson had cuts on his hands and wrists.

Initially, John Watson claimed his wife shot herself, while in the shower, yet did it in a way that would make it look like he did it. He claimed his wife, who was right handed, purposefully shot herself using her left hand, which he claimed would implicate him as the shooter. He had no choice but to cut up her body, put it in trash bags and place it in the back of his 2001 Jeep Grand Cherokee.

It is said Watson asked for a remote ground floor room at the Tuscany Suites Hotel. Their security tapes show him checking in and making reservations wearing a fake wig and mustache. Hotel records showed Watson used his keycard 15 different times in the middle of the night.

In spite of the evidence, as recorded by the *Daily Bulletin*, Watson states "I did not kill my wife. I did not hire anyone to kill my wife. I did not see my wife killed. I'm not saying she's dead or alive. I'm saying I did not do it. In my opinion, I know there are two suspects. I did not do anything, in my opinion, to cause the death of my wife."

John Watson went on a trip with his wife to Las Vegas, yet he returned without her. He did not search for her. He claims she vanished. The Watson kids reported their mom missing a few days after their father returned without her.

Watson was reported to have thanked his neighbor Gloria Donohue for keeping an eye out for his kids—while he was out allegedly discarding evidence. Donohue claimed she was concerned he would come back to town. She ordered metal security doors for her home. The trial also brought out some disturbing details from John Watson's past. In the late 60's Watson confessed to murdering a female hitchhiker. He claimed he picked her up, killed her and buried her in the Arbuckle Mountains of Oklahoma. Her body was never found and the case was dropped. Watson had also been convicted of arson in Dallas, where he set his own house on fire and eventually received a two year prison sentence. Further, Watson kidnapped his 3 year old son, from his former wife, and demanded money from his wife's parents in return for the child. Around that same time The Secret Service had charged him for threatening the life of President Richard Nixon.

John Watson has a clear record of unstable behavior. According to the newspaper, the Watsons had a somewhat normal relationship. They had not been fighting. They had not been arguing.

There had been no calls to the police for domestic battery. Residents in their neighborhood had not been startled nightly as they sat down for dinner or the evening news. A police official replied, when asked about warning signs: "No, not that we know of."

As Told by an Accused Murderer to a Writer

John M. Watson III/02592217
4L34S/04/CLARK COUNTY DETENTION CENTER
330 SOUTH CASINO CENTER DRIVE/LAS VEGAS, NV 89101
Dear John,

I hesitated to write you until your hearings were over. I didn't want to bother you during the ups and downs and stress of your trial. It's been a long stretch since we first met, where we briefly shared a classroom at the high school. You allowed me to come by for a judo workout from time to time—I still appreciate that. You did a great job with those kids—I know many of them are still involved with judo.

Over the past few years I have followed your case, and taken the time to collect some notes and ideas so I can write your story. As you might remember, I teach English, but I'm also a writer. I have done a fair amount of political writing, some promotional articles, and some website work. At any rate, I want to put together a story, or book, about your life. But, I want to do it from your perspective. I want to make sure I don't present your life from only what others have reported. I would like it to be your story. I'm hoping that you have some desire to tell that story.

Now that the trial is over, I'm hoping you will want to give more details about some of the events of your life. What happened to the mysterious hitchhiking girl earlier in your life? What are some of the details of your wife's death? Where is the body? Or, can you outline your thinking as you planned and executed any of the more compelling events of your life? Are there some sides to your life you wish people would place more focus? I hope I am not being overly candid, and I, of course, mean no disrespect by being so direct. And again, I hope that you are excited to get your story out there, in print.

John, I look forward to hearing from you.

Sincerely, Douglas

*   *   *   *   *   *   *

Thursday Aug. 21, 2010

Hello Douglas,

Thank you for your patience and respect that you paid me by not writing earlier. And I do remember you. I suspect you have followed my case from the newspapers and articles written by Rod LeBegue. His articles I have seen and they are filled with errors of my past. I offered to discuss it with him and he came here to CCDC but he only wanted to discuss my present case. I will begin with the past.

In 1967, June, my first wife ran off with our two year old boy and her boyfriend. She went to another state and became pregnant. She later broke up with her boyfriend and returned to Dallas, Texas. While she was gone, I went to Denison, Texas to try to find her. I didn't know about her boyfriend at the time. While I was gone a fire caused about $600 worth of damage and destroyed my judo gi. When I returned I called the fire department and told them it was arson. They already knew that. They asked me to take a lie detector test and I agreed. Before the test the Texas Highway Patrol verified my car was parked in Denison at the time shortly after the fire; thus, they did not give me the lie detector test.

Then in July or August, my then wife went to the judge. She told the judge that I was going to take our son away from her and that I had set our house on fire. He had me arrested and put me under a $100,000 peace bond. Thus from Aug. 1967 until the last week of Dec. 1967, I was in the Dallas County Jail with my attorney trying to help me. My attorney had the jail announce on the public address system that he could not help me and thus he withdrew from my case. I felt like I was vegetating in that jail.

In Jan. 1968, there was an article in the Dallas Times Herald about a girl kidnapped in May 1967 off of a street in some city or town in Oklahoma. It occurred while I was in a class at the University in Denton, Texas. Since I was never absent or late to any class I knew I had an air tight alibi, so I confessed the murder of the girl. I waived extradition and went to Oklahoma. I thought this would get me out of Texas and allow me to avoid the arson charge. As soon as we crossed the bridge, I told the detectives what I had done. They were able to check my alibi but the rub was that they took me back to Dallas instead of letting me go in Oklahoma.

My [first] wife was trying to get me out as she was going to have a baby, but she told the judge not to let me go unless I pled guilty to the arson. I went before the Judge and eventually I was coerced to plead guilty and receive two years' probation. I broke the probation, kidnapped my son, and fled to Colorado, then Mexico, then Belize, then Guatemala. I invited my [first] wife to come to Guatemala and she refused.

I was going to arrange, through the church, to leave my son with a millionaire while I went back to the United States to do my 2 years in prison. My son fit right in with his family. But, when I began arranging for returning to the U.S.A. with the U.S. consulate, I went into their office on a Thursday and two Secret Service agents detained me. After 4 hours they felt like my wife's claim that I was planning on killing President Johnson while he was in Guatemala was only an effort on her part to get our son back. They released [me] after that 4 hours. That convinced me to stay in Guatemala. I began teaching English (ESL) for those who already spoke some English.

Then my [first] wife came to Guatemala and got our son back. I went to her hotel and took him back forcibly. My son held onto my neck as we went down from the second floor. Then friends helped us to El Salvador, Honduras, Mexico, and Ft. Worth, Texas. I began talking on the phone to my wife but we had no reconciliation.

I was arrested in Jan., 1968. That was the last that I saw of either my [first] wife or son. By the way, my mother-in-law in early 1968 told me that her friend, Ralph Thompson, had a friend of his burn my house in 1967, while my wife was out of state in 1967.

While I was in the Dallas County Jail in 1968, I was investigated for having threatened the life of President Nixon. Nothing happened because I did not threaten any President. When I was released from prison in July, 1970, I went to Calif. to finish my education.

What you do not have is what my wife of the 1960's claimed in the penalty phase of my trial.

1. I was physically abusive to her but the police thought she was crazy when she reported it.
2. I took her to Oklahoma and almost was going to kill her.
3. That I told her the day before, that Kennedy was going to be killed.
4. That I told her to watch T.V. to see when Jack Ruby would kill Lee Harvey Oswald.
5. That I know Jack Ruby from the Carousel Club. This was only true that I was a runner for a company and I was sent to his club, once, for my company.
6. That I kidnapped our son and for money. No custody!
7. That I went to Central America to conquer it. I didn't even speak Spanish, at that time.

If you had been at my trial you would know much more. After the D.A. finished his guilt phase we had a 15 minute break. During that time, my attorney told the judge and me that he would not call any witnesses and that if I testified, he would not ask me but one question. He would not ask any of my 135 questions already prepared by me. The Power Point presentation would not happen. That the three witnesses that had contact with my wife after she was supposed to be dead, after I was arrested—would not be called. One had known my wife for over 9 years, another talked to my wife, and the third served her food and picked her out of a picture line-up given to her by the police. There is more to that witness but I am not going to talk about it.

The D.A. lied, two police officers lied, and I can prove all of this. My wife wrote a going away note and nobody will check the handwriting. Although I do not remember buying the band saw, I must have but it was not for an evil purpose. Also, I do not know where it is.

It is hard to believe that my wife would still be alive after 4 years, but I do not have firsthand knowledge of her being dead. They found Jaycee Dugard after 18 years, a man in Australia with family that missed him

15

for 25 years, a woman found in a Swiss town after being missing for 12 years, and so on. I do know my wife would not purposefully be away from our kids this long.

My attorney explains to me that he wants to win the case on appeal. This is by loopholes and that is not, and was not my wish. I had 31 witnesses that my attorney refused to subpoena for me. He pointed out that if, as said by the D.A., I had cooked my wife then why was their no human DNA on any utensils. The states witness was proved to have lied but my attorney did nothing. Did I have ineffective counsel? Yes, in my opinion. My desire was to prove, as much as possible, that I did not kill her. I love my wife and we had no problems except I kept secrets from her. I failed to tell her about my cancer because I love her. But it was my keeping secrets that caused her to leave.

I cannot put down all of the mistakes that are appealable but they should be on record, except for the ineffective counsel, by October, 2010, sometime.

Thus it is that there was no mysterious hitchhiking girl, no previous killing, no kidnapping, and no threatening the life of President by me. This is not to say I was an angel, and as I look at it I was probably mentally abusive to my first wife. I also did things as a juvenile, but never did I purposely do violence except for once involving my 3 year old son.

That's about all I can tell though there are lots more details of what I can talk about. Like the killing I witnessed in Japan and my fugue states. It just doesn't fit here. I possibly will go to prison next week.

Thanks for writing,
John Watson

***

C/O: JOHN MATTHIAS/WATSON   1056286

John,

I appreciate you making the effort to write me back. I have been looking into several of the ideas and situations that you provided me in your last letter. Once I get the full scope of those situations, I will share some of what I have found with you.

You mention your time as a juvenile—what was your childhood like? Did you grow up with a lot of support? Did you have a modest upbringing? How was your relationship with your parents?

I'm also interested in hearing more about the killing that you witnessed in Japan. That sounds like a fascinating story. Is there anything else you remember about that event?

Just recently, I spent some time reading O.J. Simpson's book, *If I Did It*, and it made me think about how much time you have had to think about your wife's murder over the past few years. Surely you have some theories as to what might have happened to her? If you had murdered your wife, how would you have gone about it; where would you have placed the body? Is it possible that you have been framed? Do you have enemies? Maybe if the body could be found, we would be able to get clues as to who the killer might be. From the location of your Vegas hotel, where would you have reasonably dumped the body?

Douglas

***

Hello Douglas,

Your letter came Thursday, but they didn't put [it] into my cell until after 1 am on Friday. Since our cells were flooded Thursday in the daytime my cell still had standing water. Naturally they don't care and your letter was on the floor and got wet. My cell wasn't dry until Saturday. An interesting thing occurred. I had a box on top of 7 rolls of paper (toilet). They were all 7 on the floor. All 7 were soaked to their top and the bottom of my box was soaked. The rolls were in ¾" to 1" of water. I am beginning this letter on Monday 11:44 am and the rolls are still wet. I am surprised the rolls absorbed water to their tops and beyond. Two of my boxes were ruined and an officer told me that they will be replaced for free. Boxes cost $7.00 each.

I have tried since Sept. 1, 2010 to get legal papers from my trial lawyer. They were in 33 manila envelopes. In them was your address, so I got my first envelopes in March and the last 2 envelopes came in on Friday, May 4, 2012. That's a wait of about 19 months. In those envelopes was the proof showing officers lied from Ontario Police Dept. Also, that the DA did not tell the truth in his summation at my trial. What he said was highly prejudicial. I just don't know if he lied or was mistaken, but in any event it was not true.

Apparently I wrote to you before March 30th, as new information has occurred, since then, that you are not aware of.

Part of what I am going to tell you can be verified with my Judo Sensei. I did not go to the Judo Club at any time in June of 2006. This was sworn to during my trial. The state's main witness claimed I talked to him about my cancer and my wanting to kill my wife in either June or May, 2006, on a Saturday. You can check with my Judo Sensei. I was not there on either Sat. the 17th or 24th as there was a Steve Bell Clinic on the 17th and a tournament on the 24th. My son was injured during final exams at school on the 13th of June so he didn't go to judo, and with my bad leg I didn't go to judo class without him. I was in a hospital on June 3rd and my son was not allowed to do judo during final exams so we didn't go on the 10th of June. That leaves May.

We did not go on Sat. May 27th. That was the day of the Memorial Day Parade in Claremont. If we had gone that day, my son would have been in the parade. He wasn't in the parade. Videos and pictures would show that.

Another problem with that date is: (1) the state's main witness was not talking to me and had not since I offended him in February, 2006. He mentioned that during the trial. (2) Why would I tell him about my cancer when I had told nobody else about it.(3) I did not know about my cancer until June 15th, 2006, nearly a month later than when he claimed we talked. (4) I was not given my biopsy until June 9, 2006, three weeks after we could have talked.

The state's main witness lied and I know lie detector tests are not reliable, but the police should have given him one.

There was a valid reason for my having the hotel I had in Vegas, but I have not and cannot tell anyone why until my retrial. My private attorneys from Sept. 2007 until June 2010 all told me not to tell them what happened and why.

From July 16th, 2006, until June, 2008, I thought my wife had died at the hospital parking lot on June 12th. I was seeing two doctors, one in jail, the other outside (in May and June, 2008). By June 10th, I realized my wife was not dead at the hospital. In August, I found another witness in the Ontario area that had contact with my wife and family for over 20 years. They have confirmed my wife was alive days after she was supposed to be dead.

The other two witnesses that also had contact with her days after she was supposedly killed are not proof. However, there is the video of my wife in Baker, Calif. It was destroyed by the Ontario Police.

Why you may ask didn't any of these facts above help me at my trial. That's a reasonable question. The reason is that my 1st chair lawyer refused to present any evidence or call any witness. He refused to prove the state's main witness was lying. Yet, the 2nd chair believed that my wife was on the security video in Barstow, but the 1st chair refused to show it.

There was no opening statement, no evidence or witness called, and the 1st chair did not give the summation of the defense. He left that to the 2nd chair to do. He was not prepared for my trial!

Now an update: I had a biopsy at Kaiser on June 9th, 2006. The urologist wrote me a note or letter saying "You definitely have cancer." I had another biopsy on Feb 26, 2012. The result of that biopsy was that they did not find any cancer.

My attorney came to see me on Friday March 30th and he told me he had filed my appeal on March 22, 2012. The strangest part of my appeal is that they dismissed a prospective juror, according to the state, because she was a Jehovah Witness. She had said she could not impose the death penalty or any penalty.

My sons have frozen all of my savings, so I cannot hire a private attorney. That is the reason I am so late in my appeals. Maybe I should have a web site that asks for funds like the guy in the Trevon Martin case that is asking for financial help. With a public defender I cannot do that plus my case is no longer an important case to the general public.

Next, in 2003, I had a growth in my left leg behind the knee. This caused me to not do any normal kneeling and made me fall a lot. In April, 2012, that growth disappeared. As a Muslim, I can now kneel and bow my head in respect to God. That leg is getting stronger and in my cell I can walk short distances. I still carry my cane just in case I am about to fall. I do not get to go outside for exercise.

Also, another appeal had been done on March 22nd. It will probably succeed. It will recall the entire district attorney's office in Las Vegas. My old D.A. claimed I stole my wife's cell phone after she died on July 11, 2006. He claimed that I lied and that I was calling my phone from her phone on July 12th.

He claimed I set her phone down in Jean, Nev., and pushed a button to make her phone dial my cell every 30 seconds. He stated that exactly four times in his summation, and that I went to Vegas to answer my cell phone, acting like she called me. There are two errors in his statements besides that I know I talked to her. There were 15 calls altogether. The first 14 calls came from 31490 S. Las Vegas Blvd., Las Vegas, NV. Cell tower 313. The last call came from Jean, Nevada, Cell tower 249. Different towers are usually a large distance apart when not in the city. I have a map of tower 313, but it does not compare tower 313 with where tower 249 is. I cannot say for certain where the two are in comparison to each other. However, my maps of 313 indicates it is near Primm, NV. That's about 50 miles from Vegas. Jean is 10 to 20 miles north of Primm. You can get a road trip map to show how far they both are from 149 S. Las Vegas Blvd., Las Vegas, NV. 89101 and see for yourself the distance apart the two towers are. If you do that please send me a copy under the Legal Mail Confidential sign on the front of the envelope. They will open it but I will get it.

The other thing that shows he erred is the time between hang ups and redials. I think automatic redial means your phone dials and if there is no answer (or a busy signal), your phone will wait a period of time, the D.A. said 30 seconds, and then redials the number. No proof that her phone had that feature, but I assume that it did. The time for the 15 calls would have been 14 x 30 seconds, or 7 minutes. This is hardly the needed time to drive the 30 miles to Vegas from Jean, NV. This in fact took from the 1st call at 7:47:13 am until 8:28:46 am, a total of 41min 15 seconds. That is not 7 minutes, hence a contradiction to his hypothesis. In geometry, proof by contradiction shows his hypothesis is flawed. But there is more.

The time between the calls, which I have at this moment in my hands, were 34 sec, 27, sec, 30 sec, 43 sec, (which supports his time of 30 sec.) but now the 5th call was 2 min 11 sec, then 4 min 23 sec, 27 sec, 30 sec, 26 sec, then 5 min 17 sec, 35 sec, then 3 min 42 sec, 34 sec, and the only call I knew of receiving 20 min 44 sec. That last call had to come from my wife and not an automatic dial. Also, when I prove she was still alive that also makes his belief wrong. I think he did not believe it and he lied.

Between July 12th noon and July 15th early am, I kept only one memory until June 10th 2008. I still do not remember buying the band saw, but I know I did and I know my wife, Eve, was still alive. We had been very active that night and morning, before I bought the saw we both had gone to our room that Thursday morning. My son would know why I bought the saw if someone reminded him.

My father was overly abusive to my brother and me. My mother was cold hearted, but then I was a problem child. She and I didn't get along, mostly for my wrongs and that she was highly prejudiced while I wasn't. I made her extremely angry because I said yes sir and yes ma'am to all races. She fell in love with Eve and that helped change her.

Let me start this part in 2007 and then go to 1946.

In the Las Vegas jail a prisoner found a book about Vegas (fictional book) that ended with werewolves. In the book he found a word that described why I couldn't remember from July 12, nor on July 15 in the early a.m. The word to describe my condition was fugue. Now go to 1946. The time between Hayaika (where I saw the girl shot in the head), and Junction City, Kansas was when I was in a fugue state of mind [a state or period of loss of awareness of one's identity, a disturbed state of consciousness in which the one affected seems to perform acts in full awareness but upon recovery cannot recollect the acts performed]. What I know about that time was told to me in the 1990's. I must have passed out. I was in the hospital, awake, and speaking fluent Japanese. Because we lived off base, my mother was afraid that rioters would come to our house and kill us. She arranged to flee with my brother and me to the U.S. on a ship. We got to the U.S. and went to Junction City. I have no knowledge of that. In 2004, my son and I did a Judo Goodwill Tour of Japan. I left the group and went back to Hayaika by myself. It was one city in 1946, but had grown to be with 6 other cities. By luck I found a woman owner of a grocery store who contacted her mother and we rode around until we found my house of 1946. I didn't tell them about the girl. I had hopes it would bring back my memory but it didn't. Except for knowing that an American shot the girl, I don't know anything else. That was in 1946. In the winter of 1947 or early 1948, I lived in Traverse City, Michigan with my brother and father [who took the kids and left my mother behind]. Our house blew up with all 4 walls knocked down and the roof lifted to the other side of the front wall. The newspapers covered it and, thus, my mother in Dallas, Texas found out where we were.

In 1956, I decided to kill myself. My best male friend had done it. I went to Gainesville, Texas, sat down in a cemetery, put the rifle to my head and pulled the trigger. The 1905 riffle's firing pin was a nail filed down. It misfired leaving an indention on the shell. I was too afraid to do it again and went into a fugue state of mind. I have only one memory during that time—when I woke up. Although, I do know what happened from being told. I was turned over to the juvenile authorities of Dallas. I had not broken any laws since the car I used was the family car. The rifle was mine. They turned me over to the state school in Gatesville, Texas. They sent me to Austin State Hosp. That was from May 1956, until June, 1956. They gave me insulin shock treatment.

In 1958, I had a good job and took a vacation. Even though I didn't speak Spanish, I went to Mexico City. While there I did something wild, and while asleep in the Hotel Mina in downtown Mexico City, the police came in holding big pistols, probably 45's, and took me to the street to their jeep. I had to pay them $1 each ($4 total) and they let me go. I don't remember going back into the hotel. I remember crossing the bridge with somebody at Laredo, Tex., an elevator at my church where I was going to kill myself, a detective choking me and then saying I was crazy and then waking up at Rusk State Hosp. in Rusk, Texas. I have records here from when I was arrested July 26th, 1968 and my trial of

Sept 26, 1968. I don't know when I was in Mexico City, nor when I arrived at Rusk State Hosp. I woke up the day I arrived at Rusk.

No memory has come back on any of my fugue states except the Vegas ones. The Vegas ones came back only after I was outside and saw things.

I know absolutely, I did not kill my wife. I do not know where she is or even if she is dead. Until June 10th, 2008, I thought she had died, in spite of the witnesses in Baker and Barstow. And, I thought I had hidden her body. I was wrong. Eve was 240lbs and I was 172-180lbs. With my bad leg and her being in the back seat of the car, where could I put her? Obviously, the band saw could not have been available in my car, and nowhere has there been any indication of the band saw being used. A butcher, in jail in Vegas, told me it could not be used on a 5'2", 240lbs animal. Plus band saws leave a lot of blood splatter. You can go to a butcher shop in your own city and verify what I am saying. My trial attorney was to have brought an actual 9" band saw to show how silly an idea it was.

You can go to Unsolvedmysteries.com and look up amnesia. They had, on the show, a story of Patricia Carlton, who had amnesia for 26 years, all as an adult. In another case they showed a woman who disappeared for 12 years because she did not want to be with her family, and they showed a man in Australia who disappeared from his wife and 2 young sons for 25 years. I know what the probability is, but I can have hope. All is possible that God chooses to be.

As far as being framed there are only three people that come to mind. If she is dead one is not probable. That is the karate instructor. He has accused me various times of stealing a mat from him. I proved that the mat had been donated to me.

A second person I can think of would not have killed my wife, but if she died he would like to have me convicted of her murder.

The third person is the state's main witness. He is framing me. I do not mean he killed my wife, but his lies have been the catalyst to get me the death penalty. As I said above, proof exists that he lied. I have not told anyone why he lied and if I can avoid telling his reason, I will. He did not tell anybody his story for 4 months after my wife went missing. He claimed I was capable of choking my wife to death with a judo technique. Ask my judo sensei. I have not successfully choked anybody since 1991 when I started. My forte was using my feet and holding techniques.

I have mentioned various internet places for you to go to. If you go to the cell tower locations, please, send me copies comparing their locations to each other.

Please, send your mail to the address on my envelope.

If my wife is dead and if her body is found somewhere I could not have been to, then what? There are 17 people that disappear from Vegas every day according to the *Review Journal of Las Vegas*.

Thanks for writing, John M. Waston/#1056286

Data as Told by Google Maps

The cell tower locations at 31490 S. Las Vegas Blvd, near Primm and the cell tower in Jean are 12.5 miles from each other. In densely populated areas, often towers will have a range of only a few miles, yet in less densely populated areas towers might have a maximum of a 22, or more, mile range. According to Jeff Fischback, a forensics expert from Los Angeles, two people standing at the same location, with the same carrier, can connect to completely different towers. Thus, with a phone set to redial, in an unpopulated area, a cell phone remaining in one location might be picked up by another tower, due to any type of minor signal or interference issue.

Furthermore, according to Google Maps it takes 30 minutes, at the speed limit, to get from the cell tower in Jean to 149 S. Las Vegas Blvd, where John Watson claims to have answered the final call. Of course he could have conceivably been a few miles away from that location to pick up that cell tower. There would be plenty of drive time under the John Watson timeline of 41 minutes 15 seconds.

<u>A Murder as Remembered by a Friend</u>

What was your relationship with Everilda Watson?

I was a noon aid at Bon View School. Most of us friends worked at the school; that's where most of us met. I saw her at Kohl's just a week before she was going to Vegas, but she did not say very much. She was in a rush to get some things to prepare for her trip. She said she had a great time on her vacation, with her husband, to Hawaii—which was part of her birthday gift. And, she was soon leaving to Guatemala to see her family. She did not want to go to Vegas—there was not enough time. Eve would have to rush to LAX, from Vegas, to fly to Guatemala. Her niece was just murdered by a gang—she was a teacher. Eve was going down to comfort her family. Even under those conditions, Eve was excited to go on her trip.

Did it seem like anything was bothering her leading up to the trip?

Even if something had been bothering her, I would have never known. She was very private. She never talked about any of her problems. As far as most of us knew there was never any fighting. But, of all the years that our families spent time together, he never was a part of it. When we would take the kids over to watch a movie with her kids, he would stay in his room; he would never come out to talk to the adults. When he did come out he would check on the kids. He would ask them if they were ok, and then he would go back to his room. He

26

was always very serious. He was very private. My husband never liked him. The one time they met, he would not even make eye contact with my husband. My husband thought it was very suspicious, and he thought there was something wrong with him.

Did you get a chance to talk to Eve when they were in Vegas together?

Once she was in Vegas I did not talk to her ever again. We spoke on the phone all the time, but never when she was with him. It's sad because not too long ago we were in Vegas, Eve and the rest of our friends. We had such a great time. She laughed the entire time, and we all told our stories, did our gambling, and it was so much fun—it was also a birthday trip. We all went with our big group of friends.

On her trip to Vegas with her husband they did not even go together. Her husband drove out earlier than she did. She flew out to Vegas a day later.

What type of person was Eve?

Eve was full of life. She was always happy. She loved to talk about her kids. She loved shopping. She loved cooking and playing games. She always went to the casino. She loved it. And, she went alone. They never went together. But, I don't think he cared. She never had a problem doing whatever she wanted to do. She also loved to get together with her friends and play Loteria. She always played that. She would come over and we would cook, eat watermelon, have some coffee, and eat pan dulce. We would talk and laugh, and have a good time.

What would you like to say to John Watson?

Why did you do it? Were you jealous because Eve was so young? The papers said maybe she was leaving him. But, she was not leaving him. There was no reason for this. I know Eve did not defend herself. She just stood there and let him kill her. In the relationship she would leave instead of argue. And, if there was no way to leave she would stand there and do nothing. She always gave good advice to others. She is the one that needed the advice. She hated aggression; she would have just stood there.

What would you like to say to Everilda?

I miss her. I miss Eve just standing behind me waiting for a handmade tortilla. She would stand there in the kitchen waiting impatiently to eat it. When he murdered her it hurt me a lot. I would have liked her to open up about her relationship, so I could have given her advice. I wish I could have told her to try to get away from him. I want to make handmade tortillas with sour cream, double fried black beans, smashed into cheese. I remember eating fried bananas with her— I would like to sit and eat a fried banana with Eve.

Eve as Seen through the Medium of Dream and Vision

My world is full of worry, fear, stress, and anxiety. I can't believe she is gone. I try to sleep. Finally I do sleep.

She is there in the corner, wearing her Capris, sneakers and white shirt. She is just there in the corner. She is not laughing; she is not crying—just standing there in a shirt with a colorful print on it. She is standing there, not angry, and not overjoyed. She just stands there in the dark corner of my living room and stares back at me.

Suddenly, we are walking through the desert. She is walking; I am seeing her walk. She is leading us. Everything is vivid, clear and real. The colors are soft like clay. The tan surface of the desert ground unfolds reaching into the distance, and the thin white clouds decorate the soft blue sky. There is no oppressive heat, no sweat dripping down Eve's face. She wants me to follow her. She wants me to see. She is real. This is her I am following. I ask myself if that is her, and I know it is her. This is not a world I have created in my head. You can't explain this away. You can tell me why this could not be her. You can explain the science to me. But, it is her. I know it's her because she is standing before me. She is leading me through the soft brown desert. She is showing me; she wants to show me, something. Animals are there, like birds, and other four legged animals—not because I put them there, but because they are there—they just happen to be there at the same time she is there. Nothing I have ever seen before has ever been more real than this desert and this walk with Eve.

She is speeding up. She is starting to rush to the spot. A slight gray covers the clouds and her face. She rushes to show me. She is rushing through this soft desert. She is becoming excited, and she is becoming worried, and I can't wait to see. She is going to show me where he did it. I am going to see where it happened. It is only a few more steps—I can sense it. A white glow surrounds her body brightening like a surging bulb. She looks directly into my eyes. I look back. I can see all of her hope brightening. She turns her head across her shoulders to show me… I am so close to seeing what we came so far to see. She looks out to the street sign just beyond us, just beyond us standing in the soft sand of this desert. And, I continued to focus my eyes on that street sign, that street sign that would show me where she is…but I will never see that sign. I will never know where she is. My husband, who I love, woke me from my sleep, from my walk with Eve. I have failed her. I have extinguished her hope.

I have always been able to sense things. I am always right. I knew my daughter's boyfriend was bad the first time I met him. Now I don't talk to my daughter anymore. He made every effort to hurt our family. He was bad, and he has broken up the family. Likewise, I always knew Eve's husband was bad—I sensed it. He is bad. He has broken up his family.

Have I ever seen her again? I walk to the restroom, down the hall, and I sense there is something to turn and look at. I sense it. There she is, sitting on the couch where she always sits. I think of her sitting there and laughing, like she often did. She always laughed loud—letting all of her joy out. She always had a good time. She always sat in the same spot.

I see her in that same spot on that couch, laughing loudly. I have seen her there a few times.

As Told by a Fellow Teacher

We shared a room. He had a storage cabinet in the corner of the room that when opened smelled like rotten cabbage. It was filled with sweaty judo equipment and other random objects. Everything was smashed and stuffed together like a hoarder's living room. I would have looked there first for murder weapons. The rest of the room was pretty orderly. He was a math teacher, always calculating and solving problems. The murder of his wife appeared very poorly planned. You would have fired him for lack of judgment if you had seen the disguise he wore when he checked into the hotel room under his alias, a crooked mustache and an ill-fitting wig. What I mean to say is he appeared to have extremely poor judgment.

I'd come by at the end of the day to drop something off and he would be on his way out in his judo gi. He had a slow awkward saunter and his big belly forced his gi open like jiffy popcorn near explosion. But, his black belt cinched it all together—as though to say, "Ok, I have a big belly. I'm getting older, and I walk with a slow saunter and a bit of a limp, but this black belt makes none of that really matter." He was walking to the cafeteria, where the judo club practiced after school, to tell the kids in the club to keep their heads up on their Ukemi and to slap the mat to break their falls. He loved that judo club. He was worried about what might happen to it if he didn't find someone to take it over when he retired.

Eventually they moved him out of that classroom. The administrator told me the only way they were going to get him to clean the junk out of that cabinet was to have him move to another room. It took a while for the smell to go away, and kids kept coming by wondering where the Yu-Gi-Oh Tournaments had been moved to. He kept a pretty low profile; I didn't see much of him after that.

A Note from a Hunter and Animal Butcher

"—would you use a band saw to cut meat?"

"I use another saw for just cutting meat, but the band saw is great for cutting through bone"

As Recalled by a Student: Class of 1994

Nobody seemed to like him. He was too hard. I mean I was good at math, so I never had a problem, but I could see if you struggled with math you would be lost. He explained himself but not well enough for the below average math students. He was not helpful, and he was also super boring.

The one thing I remember most was his lip spit. He always had this string of spit from lip to lip as he spoke. And, he would go into stories—all the time—about his son and his son's judo.

The only other thing I remember about him is that he was creepy. It was nothing specific—it was just his essence. He always seemed weird, but more than that he seemed like he had something to prove. His class was always clean and orderly—he had this sort of short man's complex—like he had something to prove, with all of his judo talk and his authoritative attitude. I have this image of him, with his lip to lip spit string working out problems, always up at the front, in a monotone voice standing at the overhead projector, ink smeared over the base of his hand and on the front tail of his shirt that seemed to refuse to stay tucked in because of his big round belly. I thought it would never end.

The First Wife

Watson's first wife said she was attacked several times by Watson while they were married. On one occasion, Watson drove her to a secluded wooded area in Oklahoma. He held a revolver, behind a pillow, to her face and told her he was going to kill her and hide her body where no one could find it, like he did with the hitchhiker.

In another instance, Watson attacked his former wife, and her mother, with a gun. The attack resulted in him shooting her mother in the cheek.

In a letter, addressed to John Watson, from his first wife, she says "You may hide your illness, but you certainly are not cured. You only wear a mask. It's about time you remember yourself for the person you are. One who slept with bullets under his pillow to get close to death."

A Murder as Told by a Judo Sensei

We first met at the Covina Dojo. Then we moved over to Chaffey College, and he decided to follow me. Even when I moved over to Claremont, I said, "John, you should go open your own dojo." But, he wanted to stay with me.

He has written me several letters from prison. I've saved them all in a folder. The letters are covered with sheets of plastic, and each letter is presented in the order received. It's not very often you end up getting letters from a killer, so I keep everything—even my summons to appear.

Do I think John is guilty? Of course I do. He wants me to believe he's innocent, but I was there that day. He tries to give the argument to everyone that he could not have been at the parade, but I was there—I saw him get in his car. That's the day he talked to the State's Main Witness. Why did he talk to him instead of me? I think he knew I would take him seriously and try to talk him out of it. I would have said, "Are you serious John?" He would have been honest with me. He must have already made up his mind. Otherwise he would have talked to me. He knew his former friend, who later became the State's Main Witness, wouldn't take him as seriously as I would have.

When the State's Main Witness told me John claimed he was thinking about killing his wife, I said, "You have to go down to the police station and tell then. You have information pertaining to a murder case. It's going to be much worse if you don't tell them, or they have to come search you out." But, he felt really funny about it. It still really bothers him. This is not something he would want to get involved with. I wish John would have told me instead. If he would have said, "Hey, I'm not doing well. My wife… I could just kill her." I wish he would have mentioned it to me. It might have changed everything. I think I would have talked him out of it. It may have just taken him hearing some corrected logic.

Did I know his wife? She was always pleasant, saw her out at the Covina Dojo with the kids when they were little. I only saw them get in one fight, seems like it was something to do with the kids. But, they didn't seem like they argued all the time. I mean he was very controlling. Everything had to be one way—he seemed very regimented. One time our families were out to dinner, and his son called his Coca-Cola a Coke instead of a Coca-Cola, and John flipped out. He was so angry at his son for calling that Coca-Cola a Coke. I don't even know why he was mad, but it seemed really out of place.

And, that's not all. We had a guy come in the Dojo one day, over at the Claremont Civic Center, and he seemed to know John. Guy seemed a little off, a little weird. He called John by another name. Some sort of alias. Juan Martinez, or something like that. I guess he was in John's chess club. John was great at chess—won some tournaments. To be honest, I think John was a card counter, and he played chess to keep his mind sharp. I think those disguises he was caught in, on the video security tapes in Vegas, were more about his card counting than the murder of his wife. I think he already had those. You want to know how a teacher gets all that money? The guy was counting cards. I tried to ask him a little about it, but he got real sheepish whenever I brought it up.

Also, he always had a weird thing about his age. He always wanted people to think he was about ten years younger than he was. At first I thought it was because he thought the kids in his high school club wouldn't want to be taught by an old guy, but now I really think he was trying to eliminate a chunk of an earlier part of his life. I don't think he wanted anyone to know about his past—the missing hitchhiker, threatening presidents…a whole chunk of his life.

Form what he indicated, he had about a half million dollars stashed. I learned once,…the psychological concept that it usually takes "three things combined" to make someone snap. She wanted his money. I think his card counting opportunities were drying up and becoming more difficult. Also, I think he was battling his age, and I think his recent retirement was difficult for him. And, he was having problems with his wife. It could have been any three of those, but I think some combination of those pushed him into the murder.

Was he strong? Could he choke someone out? I remember when we were a little younger; we were doing some Randori, which is when you drill some slow ground work. It's supposed to be slow drilling, not too aggressive. John comes at me like an animal, and he had been around long enough to know better. He was trying to wrench my jaw, and inflict some pain. That might be ok when you're trying to win a match, but not while you're doing Randori. I had to pull him aside, and say "Hey, John what are you doing. Do you want me to do that back to you? You are a lot older than me." I was a lot better than him. His judo was not very good, when it comes down to it. He was a black belt, but it was more about putting the time in than being proficient. I mean, I think he took

34

4th in the nationals one year with four guys in his division. So, yeah—he could have easily strangled his wife, and he was strong as an ox. He was unexpectedly strong for a guy his age.

A Murder as Told by the State's Main Witness

...I still feel really funny about the whole thing.

A Murder as Told by a Son

My mom called right after she landed at the airport. She would have normally continued to call and check in during her entire trip. She was always there for us. She was the nurturing one, the emotional one. My dad was the distanced one; we had a teacher student relationship. I remember travelling together, my dad and me, and we would be together for hours, driving to El Paso or Las Vegas, or flying to Japan, and we wouldn't say a word to each other. At the time this seemed normal. I mean this is how we were. But later, after seeing how other fathers and sons acted together, I realized this wasn't normal—it was a little weird.

Even at home he was very anti-social. He would come home from work and go directly to the computer. He spent hours playing online chess, or online poker. He loved chess; he had run the chess club at school, but he was never as good as he wanted to be. He also loved poker; he played poker for hours. He was trying to teach himself to count cards. He wanted to make some money off of his math skills. Sometimes he would make me play with him, so he could practice his card counting. He was never as good as he wanted to be. He had been kicked out of Vegas casinos several times. He just wasn't that good at any of it.

Why did he murder my mom? Maybe he was trying to outrun the demons in his head? About ten days after they were supposed to be back my brother and I went down to the police station and filed a missing persons report. She wasn't answering her phone. She would never not answer her phone, or return our calls. That's just not who she was.

My dad called me from Oklahoma. He said "I can't come home now. I stepped out of my car and cut my hand." I didn't really understand what he was talking about. Apparently he had driven from Vegas to Northern California, and then out to Oklahoma, and then to Texas. He was later picked up at a bus stop.

He used to write us from jail, but after a while it was obvious that he wasn't making any sense. I mean it was just crazy talk. The facts would change, but nothing made any sense. It was crazy ramblings. He ended his letters with "I did not kill mom; I did not have her killed." That was the only thing that was consistent.

You would think there would be some warning signs—some red flags—but not really. They didn't have much of a marriage, but there wasn't real arguing or yelling. She went out and did what she wanted with her friends, and he wasn't interested…and she was glad he wasn't interested. I think she may have been waiting for me to graduate before she left him. She loved her kids. Once when I was young I had some sort of biological issue where I would tear up when I went to the bathroom, and I remember telling my mom about it. She said "Sometimes I go into the bathroom and cry too." That was something I always remembered. So, maybe there were some warning signs, but of murder, maybe divorce and unhappiness, but not murder.

And, it wasn't a money thing. They kept all the money separate. My mom worked, and my dad worked and saved. They never argued about money. It was never an issue. My dad did have money saved, but it was from working over the years. He just never spent money. He only gambled a lot the last two years. Like I said, he was kicked out of several casinos for card counting. He didn't have a gambling problem—unless you count not being very good at counting cards a problem.

He did speak with me once after he murdered my mom. It was the most I think I have ever talked to him. He said "Sorry I lied to you. Your mother shot herself. I had to cut her up because she was too heavy to carry down the elevator." And, then he sort of laughed. He was telling a fat joke about my mom. My mom was too heavy to carry— pretty funny. I was disgusted and mortified. He said "Mom shot herself in a way that made it look like I shot her." I didn't say anything to him. I was a high school kid. I didn't know what to say.

He also told me about his parents, and how his father tried to kill him by triggering the furnace to explode. But, before he was engulfed by the flames his brother ran in and saved his life. His mom, my grandmother, was a hardcore racist and hated us because of our skin color. She stopped talking to my dad when he married my Guatemalan mother. By the time she started to accept us she died. That last conversation I had with him, he told me about his past. He had never mentioned any of this before. He told me about his first wife and his other kids. He told me about threatening the president and kidnapping his other children and taking them out of the country. He told me about the prostitute hitchhiker he killed. I think he picked her out; I think he may have done this before.

A friend of mine and me are thinking about going out and seeing my dad. I have just not gotten around to it. I remember the trial. There was just a mountain of evidence against him. It was never a matter of whether or not he did it; it was just a matter of getting through all of the evidence. I know my dad's friend feels responsible for being a witness— that somehow his testimony, that my dad told him that he was going to kill my mom, is what put him away—but there was a mountain of evidence. My dad's friend, who some have called the State's Main

Witness, was accurate with his testimony, and he's a good man, and he's a friend.

You know, my dad planned most of the murder about six months before when he and I went out to Vegas together. That's where most of the surveillance video used in court came from. He left me at the Adventure Dome at Circus Circus, and he went out and bought a saw, and plastic bags, and he went out and put on what he saw as a clever wig, and he rented the extra room. The room he murdered my mom in.

Some Facts of the Case as Declared by the Court

On January 31, 2007, John Mathias Watson III was charged by Grand Jury Indictment on two Counts: First Degree Kidnapping with Use of a Deadly Weapon and Murder with Use of a Deadly Weapon. The State filed a Notice of Intent to Seek Death Penalty.

Watson said he was unhappy and feared Eve was going to divorce him and take half of his money. Watson said he was "mad enough to kill her." The State's Main Witness replied "it's cheaper to keep her." But Watson stated "no, you don't understand. I know places where they'll never find her…up on the Russian River."

On July 15, Watson checked out of the Circus Circus. He called Eve's cousin at 11p.m. that same day and declared his wife was missing. She "walked away." The cousin encouraged Watson to call the police and report her missing, but Watson refused, explaining the police would "go after him." He added that Eve's blood was in the Jeep because she cut herself with a knife while opening a package of flashlights.

At 4:09 a.m. July 16, Watson called 911 in Fontana, a city bordering Ontario where they lived, to report Eve missing. Watson explained to the 911 operator that Eve had been drinking, got upset, and walked away. Eve was not generally a heavy drinker. Watson claimed his wife called him and said she was driving back with a woman she met. He also claimed she left a note for her children, informing them she had to rush to Guatemala to aid a sick relative. The 911 operator said she would dispatch an officer if he was back in Ontario. Even though Watson was only a few miles away, he claimed he would not be back in the area for four more days.

Later that morning, Watson went to the cousin's home and showed her the note. The cousin did not believe the hand writing was Eve's. Frightened, she called one of Watson's sons to come over. The note was written in Spanish. None of the children were fluent in Spanish, and their mom had never written them a letter in Spanish in the past.

Watson's Jeep was seized and taken to the Ontario crime lab. Fifteen spots of blood were found, including the rear bumper, seat belt, a piece of cardboard, and a small square piece of fabric. The Jeep also included bleach, cleaners, rubber gloves, a large plastic tarp, razor blades, maps, a wooden cane, and two flashlights. Watson's garage produced a Wal-Mart bag containing 50/50 Prestone Antifreeze, with a receipt from a Nevada Wal-Mart; a box of Glad bags, with seventeen missing; an unused Glad trash bag in a box with a smear of blood on it; a small hair found in a trash bag; and a Stanley box cutter found in the trash bag box with pieces of human tissue on it.

Officers conducted surveillance of Watson as he rented a car and travelled roughly 150 miles to the remote desert area of Lake Isabella, California. He turned off the main road onto a dirt road. After Watson left, deputies investigated an area that looked recently dug up and found a clear piece of plastic, which was still moist and had the foul smell of a decomposing body, and contained small pieces of human tissue. The plastic matches a roll of plastic found at Watson's home. The items from his garage, his jeep, and the desert matched Eve's DNA.

John Watson checked into the Tuscany Hotel using the name "Joe Nunez." The records showed he stayed in the room before, back in June. He requested room N120, located on a corner of the building on the ground floor. The room was twenty feet away from a side exit that led to a driveway where a guest's car could be parked for loading, and there is no surveillance video on that corner of the building. Room N120 was temporarily unavailable. Instead Watson checked into room N114, and simultaneously booked the room bordering room N120. As soon as N120 was available Watson requested a room change. Watson orally refused cleaning services and kept a "Do Not Disturb" sign on the door. When the housekeeper came in to clean, after Watson checked out, she was immediately overwhelmed by an odor unlike anything she had ever smelled. There was trash everywhere, and the bed sheets were missing. Watson left several items behind, including scissors with a brown stain, a Teflon pan and cooking utensils. In a letter to one of his sons, Watson said Eve shot herself in the room. Watson claimed to have washed her body in the shower. Watson then "got things to try to cut [Eve] into small pieces... [and] cooked part of her."

Detectives also discovered a large blood stain on the carpet in the middle of the room. When they cut and pulled back the carpet the detectives smelled the odor of blood. The cement under the foam pad revealed larger blood stains that would have taken a significant amount of blood over a period of time to create, requiring a "major evisceration" of the body.

After Watson's arrest, one of his sons visited him and asked him where his mother's body was. Watson replied that he would provide a thirty mile radius of where Eve's body was if his son would put money in Watson's jail fund.

The jury returned a special verdict in which it unanimously found the murder was willful, deliberate and premeditated. The murder involved torture or mutilation of the victim.

On August 26, 2010, Watson was adjudged guilty of First Degree Kidnapping and First Degree Murder with Use of a Deadly Weapon and sentenced as follows: Count 1: Life without the possibility of parole; Count 2: Death, with one thousand five hundred and one days credit for time served.

Daybook Journal: 3/22/2010

Today one of my students came in complaining one of the more awkward kids on the wrestling team was being bullied. You don't often hear about kids on the wrestling team being bullied. As the story went on I found out he was being bullied by a kid from the drama club, a thespian. I know some of the thespians are tough, potentially, but I've seen no Vin Diesel types walking around campus with a Drama Club shirt on. Also, this bully was a kid in one of my classes. He was lanky and pasty, buy nice; he didn't strike me as a bully. I guess one never knows. Apparently this pasty thespian threw a bucket of water in the wrestlers face, leaving him very wet and uncomfortable, and then he said some unkind words to him. The pasty kid is a senior, and the awkward wrestler is an underclassmen. Ironically I don't think the wrestler is much of a fighter. He's more of a slow, pudgy, gamer.

I found myself voicing some surprise at what might motivate our pasty friend to do such a thing, and then I gave a short warm up activity and went back to my desk where I decided not to hear any of their conversations on the matter.

The next day, during passing period, several kids seemed to be grouping up around the door with what looked like water balloons. Officially I wasn't paying any attention and I had no idea what they might be up to. Unofficially I was thinking it might be better if they did this outside, or not at all. At any rate, before I could think it through water balloons were being hurled at the pasty kid, many more balloons than I would have suspected possible—immediately I thought this is a practical joke gone south. Suddenly pasty turned red and started whirling around in a circle in a Wile E. Coyote motion. I could have sworn some heat and dust was flying off of him while he spun. Then he stopped suddenly and it was obvious he was looking for someone to hit or something to destroy. Lucky for all of us, and me and my job especially, the only person left standing there, really just by coincidence, was a large football player that sits in the back row. Pasty considered it, but a momentarily clearer head prevailed.

Officially I'm convinced it was just a summer's day prank, not retaliation. In hindsight I'm convinced of it. I got in a little trouble before I left for the day, but I think we all learned a valuable lesson.

Daybook Journal: 10/20/2014

My wife has made the comment many times that my book is nothing more than a collection of incredibly negative stories. She made the comment that people are going to come away from the book feeling really negative. She wondered why, after all these years of a happy and healthy marriage and family, I see the world in such a negative way.

Why focus on these types of stories? Because, if you're anything like me, you need an almost constant reminder to wake up and live life with an aggressive sense of urgency. It's a constant battle. "The mass of men lead lives of quiet desperation"—if Henry David Thoreau's words touch you maybe this book will motivate action. I have lived, and often still live a life of quiet desperation. Yet, when I think of those having suffered in a way that forces them to alter their lives, or worse those no longer owning the chance to live a life at all, I feel shame not to live fervently and aggressively in each moment. I fail in each moment, yet honor those gone before me with constant attempts.

Some, like my loving wife, are motivated by fields of heather, baby flying unicorns, and blissful tales ending with the defeat of evil. I'm just not wired that way. If you are wired that way you might want to put this book down.

Those stories are wonderful and give us all hope. They inspire us. I have had many happy stories, amazing and inspirational people, and beautiful relationships in my life. They have all been enhanced by the knowledge life is fleeting and time is much shorter than we want to believe.

Things can turn in a moment. I'm going to work to force life to turn in a direction that would garner the respect of those rendered powerless and stifled. When my daughter asks me to play a game with her, and I'm too tired, these stories remind me only a fool waits to start living.

3

Unauthorized Account of the Christmas Massacre—Part I

Everyone's fired up. I mean it's almost Christmas—what's not to like. Seniors: they've done this many times before. This is old hat. They have this pre-vacation procedure down. Some of them will do this again in college, but it won't be the same; it won't be the public school system, where nothing will happen of any academic value this last week. We will make up a reason to have a party. But, we won't call it a party, of course. It's not even a holiday party; we refuse to offend any other religions, or to appear less academic, and less willing to apply all of our educational time to trying to raise test scores—it's a 'cultural experience,' or like last year for instance, a *Macbeth* style cultural lesson. Surely killing everyone to become king, and then meeting your own demise echoes prophesy of the holiday season, and the need for a cultural celebration.

It just so happens that it's a ceremonial King Arthur round table white wizard gift exchange. But, instead of everyone bringing foods thematic of King Arthur's day, like giant drum sticks and hemlock juice, they are bringing foods representative of their culture—you see what we are doing here? We are showing comparative examples through contrast—so, yes, because every student in this class is Mexican we will be eating tamales and tiny taco plates. They will be delicious and culturally significant. And, we will find an old something or other to wrap up from home that has a street value of roughly five dollars.

You can image the type of stuff they bring. You get about ten five dollar gift cards from Starbucks, but then you get some lotion or bath gel that has been in some girls medicine cabinet since last Christmas. Or, you get a box of condoms and a pair of G-string underwear wrapped up in newspaper. You want to punch that kid because now someone is sure to tell their mom and you are sure to get fired, lose your wife, your house, your kids, and your life.

Nick brought a sock—he called it **The Xmas Sock**, which was written across the top of the sock with a black sharpie. It was filled with some random crap—I don't even remember. What I do remember is the sock hanging from the ceiling tile for the next two years. Nick and Michael were friends. They played baseball together. They laughed together, and bet on high school football games together, and made fun of things together.

My wife made me go to the bagel shop with her and my daughter. My Christmas break was about a week from over. My wife likes to fill my vacation days with long walks and fun family things. I picked up the paper, and there it was. Michael Ortiz had been killed in the Covina Christmas Massacre. It says a man dressed up in a Santa Claus costume came into the party with a gun and a flamethrower. After shooting, and burning several people he burned the house down and drove away. "This kid is in my class. I just graded two of his papers." "What kid?" "The kid murdered in the Christmas Massacre." But, she only seemed to want to know what we were going to do after we ate our bagels. Her response made me mad and I wanted to punch her. Apparently she thinks I'm less sensitive than I am. I couldn't shake it—what a great kid. "This was a great kid…played baseball, good student, super nice."

"Now he is always going to be seventeen" she said. Her comment made me want to punch her in the face again, but because I'm an English major it also immediately made me think of a poem that had once irritated me, and somehow made it impossible for me to become a true Romantic—the one with the two lovers just about to embrace in a kiss; they are frozen in time. They will never kiss. They will anticipate the kiss for eternity. I used to think that was a very positive image. They will anticipate, with excitement—which is that the best part—the anticipation. They will never grow old. They will never experience the struggles—is that a blessing? Something seemed very unfair about that, yet for whom? The paradox is upsetting.

So this man, that killed Michael Ortiz, and massacred a dozen people at the Christmas party, who deserves no name, dresses up in a Santa suit, goes to the party where his former wife is, and he starts shooting people. He earned an M.S. in electrical engineering—or was it computer science? What's it matter? His divorce had just been finalized. Does that make a difference? She got some cash, and his dog Saki. He used to go to lunch with that dog, now he goes to lunch alone. The routine, the tradition, had been soiled. Montrose Bakery & Café with a turkey pastrami sandwich on his plate, a lonely plate of meat and bread. He can't help but look down at an angle were Saki would be, where Saki should be. Ordering the raspberry dish, why even bother? Dessert for one, it just won't do—Anger and remorse, fueled by a divorce and a wife who now loathes him and a lost job just a week ago. But, to be fair, his story started years before.

Things started off right, standing there at college graduation holding a blow up doll, smiling and celebrating. Things could not have started off better, a great job at NASA's Jet Propulsion Laboratory followed by sought after employment at medical centers and software manufactures. One acquaintance reported "He was the nicest guy. He would do anything for the church."

He was living the dream, a new wife, a fantastic house, and a beautiful child. But, his path would soon be altered. One sunny afternoon he decided to take a break and relax a little and catch up on some T.V.

The keys rattled and the grocery bags crackled as his wife shifted to set her purse down. "Hey honey! I'm home. Why don't you help me bring in the groceries?" She continued on in, set some bags on the cold granite of the kitchen island, and surveyed the room where he was slowly setting the remote down to get up and help her. "Where's the boy?" Where is the boy? "He should be out back." Panic and fear followed his response. How long had he been watching T.V.? It couldn't have been that long.

The boy is in the pool, and he's not moving. Drag his listless body out—don't waste time—too much time has already been squandered. He is alive, but unresponsive. The boy is a strange shade of gray. If only time had not been taken to stop and relax to watch T.V. If only this pool home had not been purchased, none of this would have happened! If not for this, this man may have never been fueled with enough anger to massacre several people. He would have never created thirteen orphaned children when he shot and burned their parents with a pistol and a home-made flamethrower at the Christmas party.

Sitting and hoping by his son's bedside for an entire week, he prayed. God you have to fix this! Absolve me of my guilt. If only he could take it back. He swears he would do anything to take it back. He will do anything; just fix the boy. But, it would not be. The boy will live, but he will have brain damage; he will be a paraplegic. God never gives us more than we can handle. Yet, we all handle things in our own way. You are blessed; he will live. I will grant you your prayer. But, that was not the prayer. If you can't fix him, he would rather the boy die. His guilt is too heavy. He decides he will never see this child or its mother again. The only connection he maintains with his former family is using the boy as a tax write off for the next seven years.

Over time, he remarries and his new wife finds out about his past, and she just can't live with it. He thinks they can work it out, but she feels betrayed and blindsided in this marriage to a man she now feels she never really knew. He becomes enraged. This was supposed to be his do over. Now it is all falling apart. She claims the marriage is over and their differences are irreconcilable. He decides the only solution is to kill his wife. She must die. Enough is enough. This life has wronged him. She won't get away with this. She can't get away with this. Her belongings shall be found piled up and scattered in the street. She thought that would be the worst of it. She thinks that's the end of it?

He is patient and makes a calculated revenge plan. He ordered the Santa costume months ago. A large man must special order, and there must be some extra room for hand guns and tanks of CO_2 and racing fuel. Guns take time to buy. You can't just go into a gun store and buy five Sig Sauer 9-millimeter hand guns. You have to wait 30 days between purchases. Five months later: nine hand guns, tanks and hoses, a functioning compressor, and an extra-large Santa suit. As well as, a trip to a friend's house in Iowa where one can buy 16 handgun magazines instead of the eight that California allows.

Time to get ready...the devil is in the details. Put on the boot covers, slide on the belt, straighten the beard, slip the gloves on and double check the plastic glasses—just a little cocaine to take the edge off. Oh yeah, that's it. The door closes behind him. He is focused and committed. "Where you headed off to?" asks his neighbor. "Going to a Christmas party!" He gets into a rented blue Dodge Caliber, and the neighbor wonders why he would rent a car to go to a Christmas party. A while later his brother pulls up to pick him up. It turns out they had plans to go to a different party that night. But, he finds there is nobody there to pick up.

It's dark as he drives up. He's not conflicted. It's pure rage and planning, built from a warped sense of jealousy, envy and the unfairness of this world. Not sensible thoughts, but the kind of thoughts that are confused in the mind, a distortion of thought. Like love when it transforms itself into rape after being filtered through the mind vacuous of moral logic.

Did he get out of his car slowly and methodically, or did he get out quickly and excitedly. Adjusting his Santa belt, pulling the makeshift tank of vapor and fuel out of his back seat, strapping it on, making sure it was adjusted correctly, his hand in the optimal trigger pulling position—that it was disguised properly enough to be confused for a Christmas gift, in a way allowing him to draw his guns while holding or accessing his home-made flamethrower.

He walks up to the house and knocks on the door. It's noisy inside. Partygoers are involved in noisy drunken conversation. He waits patiently to kill the laughter and joy with calculated rage.

"M'ija, get the door." Jumping up quickly moving to the door, propelled by the excitement of the season, and the anticipation of opening gifts with unknown contents, the eight year old girl opens the door. Might it be that one neighbor that always comes dressed as Santa—could this be him? That Santa was out of town. This Santa lifts the gun, and he pulls the trigger. One shot to her small delicate face, cutting through her tiny jaw. Shot in the face she runs and she escapes. The little girl moments later, her face filled with tears and blood, stands in the kitchen of the neighbor's house as her mom makes the call to 911. "He's shooting my whole family! He's shooting, he's shooting, he's shooting…my mom's house is on fire! My daughter has been shot in the face. And, a curse has fallen upon us all."

After he shot the little girl in the face, he moved forward and continued shooting. People scattered. He lifted his gun, aimed, fired, and shot a bullet into the back of an escaping girl. Another jumped in panic hiding behind the couch. Others ran upstairs. He continued to shoot at anyone in his line of vision. He shot the running and executed those that didn't flee fast enough. As he walked, he fired dual 9 millimeter handguns, fired with both hands until his clips were empty, then he dropped his handguns, and he reached for the hose of his flamethrower tank. He continued to walk and spray vaporous gas from his tank. He walked around patiently fumigating every corner with flames and gas.

Some escaped by smashing through windows. One girl desperately jumped from the second floor and mangled her ankle, but she was alive. Another ran into the backyard, trying to climb the back wall to freedom. Jumping and scratching at it, getting over the wall with the help of the neighbor. "There's some guy shooting in there!" According to this neighbor, the family dog frequently escaped from this yard. Now the entire family was escaping.

As smart as Santa assumed he was, his plan was partially thwarted. The vapor from the CO_2 and racing fuel erupted. Was it a candle, a pilot light, or one of the fireplaces, burning their Yule logs? The explosion slammed into him with a wave of incredible heat. The plastic wrap that held his escape money tight to his body, beneath his girdle curled, bubbled and singed at the edges, melting into his flesh. His Santa suit melted into his arms, as it became one with his skin. On his way out his fake plastic glasses and Santa hat dropped from his charred body.

The killer exited the home and as he left, according to a neighbor, he knocked out the street lights. They locked their doors, and watched him slowly get into his Dodge Caliber. He drove slowly away with his headlights turned off.

He decides to drive to his brother's house in Sylmar. He was badly injured, and his master plan to flee the country after these brutal murders had been destroyed. He rigs his Santa suit with a trip wire that would ignite a flare, which would ignite black powder. It would be his final act of revenge upon this cruel and unfair world. His hope was to blow up those coming for him, along with his airline tickets, his money and himself.

In his brother's living room—defeated—he shot himself in the mouth. His body collapsed to the floor, folding over itself to the ground. Lying there in defeat, guns fallen by his sides—with his wedding ring still on his hand—with nothing.

Back at the party the firefighters were held back because of reports of gunshots. Could they have done anything to help the victims? By now the fire would not be stopped before the heat of its embers destroyed the supports of this house, allowing the roof to collapse inward. Two hand guns were found in the ruins. Bodies were found—charred to the point they were not recognizable.

The fire burned for hours. Initially police couldn't get into the house. They had no idea how many people had died. Meanwhile, a dad searches the bushes frantically calling for his son. "Michael, Michael...Michael! Michael, come out!" A shadow—and a glimpse of hope—a clump of branches that might be hiding something—and a glimpse of hope— another set of hedges—and a glimpse of hope, a sick feeling in the stomach, a building anxiety that tops off and begins to turn into fear and hopeless, lifeless despair, yet hoping at any moment he might see his son and a feeling of relief might overcome him.

Michael Ortiz was allegedly alone in an upstairs room. When school started back up after Christmas break, the counselor went into every one of Michael's classes. What does she say? Is there something to be said? Or is it so overly perfunctory that it makes everything worse for everyone.

"For some of you wondering how Michael died—he went very peacefully. He was probably asleep upstairs. He told his family he was going upstairs to sleep after going on the computer for a while. Even if he was awake as it started, the smoke would have put him to sleep before the fire reached him. I can assure you he died peacefully. If any of you have any questions—please come and talk with us. We can help you get through this."

Michael, did you die peacefully, like a candle slowly burning out? Or did you hear the gun fire, look out the door and see your family being massacred? Did you hide in a closet? Did you put a towel under the door as the flames approached? Did you cry when the flames reached you? Did you pass out before the flames became so hot your flesh began to burn away? No, I'm sure the counselor is right; I'm sure it happened like she said it did. She is old, and she knows things. We are best to trust what she says.

The coroner said later he could not be sure what the victims had died from. They died. We can be certain of that—most of them not peacefully—nobody dies of thermal burns, gunshot wounds, fire caused by the explosion of flammable gas, and smoke inhalation peacefully.

I didn't create a special lesson plan for that first day back. Maybe I should have, but I knew there was no lesson plan for this.

Time simply won't freeze for any man.

Unauthorized Account of the Christmas Massacre—Part II

—An interview with Michael Ortiz based on arguments taken completely out of context from what were most likely some of the last words he ever wrote.

Michael knew about presentation and reality. He had written about it in his studies of Machiavelli; he had studied it when he wrote his analysis of Lady Macbeth. Michael argued that …*everyone can see how you appear but few can feel what you are.* Does this apply only to the villainess, Lady Macbeth? Who could have truly known what this man was? Surely, not an eight year old girl opening a door? Yes, the Santa Clause Killer had a history of problems, but should we have the deep insight to be prepared on this level. Santa Claus made himself at home. He came in and looked to the right and the left. He raised his gun. Then he walked carefully around and shot as many people as he could.

Something was not right with this man. How could this be understood? How do you make sense of this Michael?

[He] *Tried to destroy everyone who was not like [him] by any means necessary…. Machiavelli as a leader thought war was necessary and that one should be ready for it at all times. He said, "It is necessary for the prince to use the ways of beasts. He should imitate the fox and the lion…"*

But, Michael, this man was no leader. He was no fox; he was not a real lion. But, he did have problems and…

…*you have to shape your plans out to best solve the problems presented to you. In his mind [he] had to approach an attack with a strategic plan in order to win.*

This was a plan, Michael, and it was strategic, but how can this man feel that he could win? How would he feel victory?

"Men judge more by their eyes than by their hands. Everyone can see but few can feel. Everyone can see how you appear but few can feel what you are" (Machiavelli).

The counselor came in to soothe all of your friends' nerves, but I can tell you that your friends had no interest in her stories. I think you're right when you say *...the news might display a certain event, the people judge more because of what is only shown on television, newspapers... They never really endure the event hands on or experience it first person; it is like they brainwash you to believe what they want you to believe.*

What would you say to them Michael; what would you say to your friends that won't be seventeen for all eternity?

"...as human beings we are self-determining. Adler says "life is movement" ...we shape our own destiny. Dewey stated that, "We not only react—we act; therefore we can change."

But Michael, this man changed your destiny, stopped what you were becoming.

Dewey also said, "We are goal-directed. We are not pushed by causes, but rather pulled by goals and our dynamic striving causes usually cannot be changed, but goals, once they are recognized, offer a choice."

Didn't he not stop all choice? Where is choice now?

...you can't always get what you want no matter how hard you try.

If it's not too late for us, what is our approach...before our time here is over? What should we strive for?

"The first understanding is that we, all people, of all ages are socially embedded" (wiki.com). This is based on beliefs that the human race are *"social beings"... whose main goal is to find where we belong and how we can fit in.*

What sense does any of this make?

"There are two types of fighting: one with laws and the other with force. The first is most suitable for men, the second is most suitable for beasts" (Machiavelli). *[This] Means that men that like to be aggressive are known as beasts and men that use justice and laws are men's men.*

This man was a beast.

According to the basic principles of classical Adlerian psychology, Lady Macbeth [as was the Santa Claus Killer] is mentally crazy due to severe ambition and greed. …masculinity from within is what drove [them] to madness and eventually violence. She is going insane and does not show any remorse to the deeds she has done in order to gain power and respect. All she worries about is her status, her rank throughout the people. She wants to belong…

But she, like the Santa Claus Killer, will never right wrongs. Even if the world has treated them with unfairness, they can never go back. Time can't be rewound.

"A little water clears us of this dead" (Act II, Scene ii, 65). …completely blind to all the guilt [they] should be feeling and as a result [they] descend into madness.

Just as the Santa Claus Killer could not end his madness—it was almost as if this was his destiny. Maybe the witches of Macbeth were right? Our destiny is set; there's nothing we can do to change it.

If you also notice there are times when she does not speak in verse she fades away from iambic pentameter format. This goes to show her mental and emotional state is heading forward—to insanity. Lady Macbeth notices the chaos she is causing but yet she does not react with any regret or shame. Instead it drives her to do more evil deeds.

I see the parallel. Would there have been a way to change course, to change their destiny?

As a recommendation I would have suggested that Lady Macbeth, [and the Santa Clause Killer], to have talked over [their] ambitiousness to someone that might listen and help understand it was uncontrollable. Through counseling [they] might realize not every terrible act needs to be carried out. [They] might also be told by someone you can't always get what you want, no matter how hard you try. Maybe then [they] could come to a normal state of mind and ease off of [their] greed and obsession to have the throne.

The answer is counseling?

Yet, maybe it is too late. Shakespeare concludes best when he says, "The raven himself is hoarse, that croaks the fatal entrance of Duncan, ….Stop up the access and passage to remorse…Nor Heaven peep through the blanket of the dark to cry" (Act I, Scene v, 36-52).

Daybook Journal: 5/2/2013

I've had lunch every day with Luis and Mr. Sims for the past seven years or so. We talk about investing, sometimes our shared students, and sometimes our big plans for the summer. Mr. Sims is big on 3D printing stocks, and he assumes he's going to ride those, along with his underpriced blocks he picked up of Bank of America, into his amazing retirement package, bundled along with his real estate and retirement pensions from his varied construction careers. I sometimes will retell the story of the Starbucks stock I picked up at just over $3.00 a share, which I sold early to become even more heavily invested in ABK…which was a mortgage loan insurer now worthless and dissolved. If I would have only held Starbucks… what could have been? Luis is more of a buy and sell trader. He likes to track stocks that go down, where he buys, and then pop back up regularly, where he sells. Or he takes some risks with some Options trading.

Luis will often repeat a joke he overheard a student tell. Usually these jokes lack insight and are about how fat your mom is, which is an easy joke because some of their moms are fat—most of them report having traditional Mexican moms who lack nutritional knowledge—there's a lot of lard, and a lot of snacking on Red Hot Cheetos and bags of Takis chips. But, the ones they tell to their friends with the racial overtones, that you listen to from a distance, because you're a trained teacher and even when you don't want to you can hear pretty much anything anybody says in the classroom, are often of some quality. There are lots of conversations you pretend not to hear. Luis said "You guys have probably heard this one, but why do Mexicans make tamales at Christmas…So they have a few things to unwrap on Christmas morning." We have heard this one before, but for some reason it's still funny. "Did a Mexican kid tell that joke?" Luis explains he thought the kid was at least half Mexican, but the other Mexican kids he told it to thought it was pretty funny.

Then Mr. Sims told us a story about one of his former students, which I couldn't understand, because it wasn't funny at all. You don't start in on a long sad story…we only have a thirty minute lunch.

4

I Think He Killed a Man

Back in the late 1990's I heard they made him remove his "flying high" bumper sticker.

I heard he lived in Europe for a while. Maybe building something for the war effort.

I heard he lived in Japan and Germany. I think they say he killed a man?

You're kidding. I bet he did kill a man!

He looks like he would kill a man.

I'm pretty sure he had a friend in the Hell's Angels. And, he won't tell anyone his birthday, but he gets mad if we don't bring him something on Teacher's Day. I always come and bring him a cake and a Starbucks Card.

People say he has a middle name, but nobody knows what it is.

I bet he killed a man.

Mr. Sims teaches Masonry. You know the bricks and mortar. The Masonry Program builds all of the memorials. They built the frog memorial when the former administrator Mr. Connor passed away. They also built the Michael Ortiz Monument out near the baseball field. They protect the planters they designed with metal clips, they created themselves, to keep the skaters away. They honor, they decorate, and they build. Mr. Sims and his crew work out in the front of the school on the new paver project that someone else will later take credit for. "Nice pavers Mr. Principal." "Thank you. We do what we can to showcase our four star school." But, it was really those dusty boys that deserve all the credit, and Mr. Sims, of course. He stands out there barking orders while wind filters smoke from his pony tail, leaving the hint of Cigarillo Swishers in the breeze.

Get those pavers going. Measure that angle. Is that level?
Yeah!
What!?
Yes Sir! I will take care of it Mr. Sims.

They work their butts off, or else. Of course, these aren't the honors kids, and once in a while a few of them make a poor choice. For instance a couple of them might slip down an alley during the job and beat the shit out of each other while a small pack of kids stand around to watch one worthless guy, kick another near worthless guy in the head while he's already on the ground.

Yet, some of them learn how to go to work, and end up making bigger paychecks than their fathers. Some of them learn to prepare themselves to take a boot to the throat. He tries to teach both. Mr. Sims will teach a skill. He will also tell a story. He spends almost a month on the safety test. If they can't pass it, they don't work with their tools. They seem to take naturally to working with their hands, lifting blocks, and hammering, piling things up, carrying items from one spot to another, opening and pouring bags of sand and mix, but some of them can't identify a picture of a saw. They are stymied by the safety test. Mr. Sims forces them to read, and he forces them to understand.

You have to know your safety rules, or you won't be able to work with your tools! You fail the safety test, you will write a letter to your parents explaining to them you chose not to study every night this week…every day for the past six weeks. What have you been doing? You'll get it signed by them, or I'll call them. You don't want me to call them.

But my dad only speaks Spanish.

Then you better get it signed.

But my parents aren't home.

You better not fail the test then dumbshit. When I worked on giant boilers guys would make mistakes. They didn't follow procedure. I've seen grown men fall in and burn to death. One time they pulled a guy out, but even if they pull you out—you're still dead. They pulled his boots off and some of his foot came off like a boiled chicken leg. He suffered and screamed for the next ten hours. Study your safety dumbshits! Or someday they will pull your boot off your chicken bone and make soup with it. And they will call it good because they'll cover it with Tapitio and eat it with a tortilla.

All kinds of kids take Masonry—the gang kids, the taggers, the petty thief, the low level dealer, the construction minded kid or the kid that just wants to learn a new skill. But sometimes a skinny nerdy kid will sign up, or a little girl that wears a Hello Kitty backpack and decorative clips in her hair. She will be sweet and naive. Nobody would call her a dumbshit—she is much too gentle.

This sweet girl did sign up for Masonry. She had been saving for a car. It was hard to imagine her driving. She was responsible of course, but she was fit better for a bicycle with a basket, tassels hanging from the hand grips. You can picture her with pigtails, two different colored plastic barrettes, riding in a circle. So, to think of her grabbing a bag of sand and getting her tape and trawl out is surprising.

A few hoodlums heard she was saving money to buy a car. They decided taking her money would be easier than learning a skill and going out and making it themselves. Yet, they found out the hard way taking money can be more trouble than earning the type of money Mr. Sims will teach you to work for. Mr. Sims had never taught these hoodlums; if he had, maybe they would have learned something. Maybe it would have been the telling of the right story on the right day that might have helped them. Maybe the speech about how there are too many quitters in this world. Or, maybe the story of all the kids that sign up for his after school class and then stop showing up—because they quit...they are quitters. Or maybe his speech about this being real life?

High school isn't real life. High school is much different than real life. If you go out and get a real job, or you decide to go to college you will see what I'm saying.

What do you mean Mr. Sims?

In college they don't baby you for every single little thing. Counselors don't call you out of class to keep reminding you about your absences or the credits you're behind, or give you a juice box when you fail a class. It's nothing close to college.

But like I said, the hoodlums never had this class. They never heard that speech. She had heard it. And, life would become very real for her. Maybe if those thieves had experienced kindness mixed with tough love, maybe it would have made an impact. Like when Mr. Sims overheard a girl in class was having a birthday and likely not getting any gifts. She had no family to speak of, so he gave her friends a little pocket change to buy some gifts—a brief class time exchange of shoes, some perfume and a small cake. It made a difference.

One story is that the hoodlums approached her when she came out of her house to go running. They wanted that money. I'm sure it sounded like an easy score. When you aren't educated or trained well enough to have a good job—and you have one where you're forced to work like a slave—even though you set the course for your own slavery, when you decided not to study for the tools test, or what have you—robbing an innocent girl sounds like an easy score. When you're an idiot in all other things—logic should tell you that you're probably an idiot in all things, legal and illegal. When you're not very smart it's easy to overestimate your ability.

Come in and sit down.

Should we get our tools Mr. Sims?

No, not yet. Get your drawings out, and we'll finish those up. You need to know the rules of measuring to get those drawings right. Rules are important. One time I had this date, with a very pretty woman. We went to dinner, and we had a wonderful time. We took a drive, and there were some orange trees in a gentleman's yard. So I turn to my date, and I said, "Did you know that any tree with fruit hanging over public property is public property?" So, I grabbed some fruit. I was, after all, picking public oranges. Then a man came out and said "Hey that's my fruit!" So, I had to explain the California law about fruit and the man tried to assault me—but that's a story for another day.

You risked your life for some fruit?

I don't know that I risked my life—I've never taken what I don't have a right to—the law is the law.

If I did that my dad would beat me.

Your dad probably should beat you. That's why I don't have any kids. I remember one day—it was oppressively hot out, and I see this dad out there...and it was Mexican desert hot. So, I'm on my way back to my car, from the store, and I see this really frustrated man by an

Astro van whose kids were getting on the man's last nerve. The kids did something—asked for another piece of Mexican candy maybe, and the man reached his boiling point and yelled "GoooootDaaaam it!!!" His accent is what made it so funny.

That doesn't seem funny!

Well, it was funny—you had to be there. I got in my car and I turned the AC all the way up, and I turned up the radio, and I don't think I have ever been happier than in that moment to not have any kids.

These hoodlums, that approached Mr. Sims's young student, didn't care about the law, or the nuances of law, or taking more than their share. They had never had a dad that cared enough about them to yell "GoooootDaaaam it," or to beat them in a loving and supportive way, nor had they been told a story about one. I mean, I have to believe they hadn't, but I'm an optimist when it comes to the power of story and experience. One of the hoodlums that helped in this crime was a Mexican native. During his trial he needed the taxpayers to provide him with a headset so the content of the trail might be translated to him. That was kind of the taxpayers to provide. We can all rest easy to know he was able to clearly hear all of the horrible things he had done before being sentenced to 15 years to life in prison. But, he did only drive the other two men to her house. I'm sure he was simply talked into it. Maybe there was a language barrier? If only the state would have supplied him with a headphone before his being asked to take part in this crime he may have understood the implications of his actions on that dark day. The girl had just come home from school after her last period with Mr. Sims.

Come in. Class is about to begin.
Do we get our tools Mr. Sims?

Just have a seat for a minute. You're always in a rush—unless it's not fun. How many of you guys have a vehicle to drive around—to go on dates?

I have a car Mr. Sims. I'm fixing it up. It doesn't drive right now.

I hope you know how to drive that thing. You know driving a car is about twice as hard as riding a bike. And, piloting a plane is four times as hard to do as driving a car, and flying a helicopter is about 10 times as hard. Flying a helicopter is so hard that piloting a plane seems so easy anyone can do it.

Mr. Sims, do you know how to drive a plane?

Bitch you don't drive a plane; you fly a plane!

The three hoodlums had never flown a plane, nor had they piloted a helicopter. These assholes couldn't even manage to save up enough of their own money to buy their own car. At least save up enough money for your own car before you start committing crimes that require use of a car. It's a work tool. Would a plumber wait a few years to buy a torch? Would a carpenter come to work with no hammer? Only a worthless one.

One of these guys dropped the other two men off on his way to work at the dairy farm. As he dropped them off one of the men opened the trunk and took out some plastic gloves. They approached the girl's home. Why her? She was unlucky enough to have worked with one of the three men. They believed she had several thousand dollars in her bank account she could be forced into giving them. The two men talked their way into the girl's house. Then they turned their attention to torturing her. They needed her ATM pin number. That was the initial focus, yet assaulting the girl was also a part of their plan. I mean this girl isn't going to be able to tell anyone. You can't just take a pin number and let a girl go. She may be sweet and innocent, but she's going to run and tell the first chance she gets. It would be a waste not to go ahead and rape and sodomize her. Before or after the raping, they took her ATM card. They also took some stereos, and collected the keys to the family Toyota. Then they set fires in an attempt to burn the house down. The house did not burn down, probably because these guys were not that intelligent. They had never taken Mr. Sims's class. It's incredibly difficult to read and research the art of carrying out effective methods and strategies for arson when you can't read or think very well.

They loaded the dying girl into the trunk of the car. Possibly they knew enough about themselves to know the fires would not be effective and to leave her body inside would be unwise. They went back to one of their homes. Then asked their driver to come back to help them get rid of the Toyota they had just stolen. They drove several miles until they found themselves in the sage brush desert hills of Jurupa. When the two cars came to the end of the paved road they stopped to talk. One of the men got in the Toyota and continued further down the now unpaved road. The other car drove down the road momentarily, then stopped and turned around to face the exit. The man in the Toyota stopped, got out and opened the trunk. The girl was still alive. Did the man have a plan for that? Did he think she would still be alive? Did he think he was stronger than he was? Possibly assuming the beatings would have done her in. But, she was alive. Did she look up into his eyes with fear? Did he hesitate?

Mr. Sims grimaced and shook back his emotion as he retold the story. I'm pretty sure he never killed a man.

The man was either lazy or tired. We already know he was stupid. If you're going to kill someone, get it done quickly—be humane about it. He didn't finish her off with his own hands. Maybe it's similar to catching fish when you're young. It's exciting when you reel the fish in. It's fighting back and lashing back and forth. Your adrenaline is pumping and you're reacting and battling. In the moment you feel like a real man. Then you get back to the camp site and its time to clean the fish, and you realize you have to take the fish in your own hands and look the small fish into its near dead eyes and you have to finish killing it. You have to clean it. I don't mean clean its dirty gills with a bar of soap. You have to take it in one hand and stick a knife in its rectum. Then, you have to slit its stomach with manly force, so when the blade gets tangled in its intestines you can bear down on the knife and cut it up to its fish throat. You can't be shaky or nervous because that knife needs to be steady so you don't cut your own fingers off. But rather than steady yourself and finish the job like a man, you leave the fish in the bucket and wait for your father or your older brother to clean it for you. That's what the killer did. He placed her weak, yet conscious, body on the ground, and he walked around to the driver's side where he didn't have to see her body, he got in and he put the car in reverse. He may have had to listen to crunching and popping human flesh, but he didn't have to kill her with his own hands. He ran over her body repeatedly…taking it out of park, putting it back into reverse, back into drive, back in reverse, back in drive.

The other man, the man that waited down the dirt road, knew everything. He knew the girl was in the trunk. He knew she was going to be killed, and he knew her life was worth the resale cost of a few stereos and the fantasy of the ATM card. But, when they went to the ATM machine they couldn't get the card to work. Had she duped them, or had they duped themselves? Either scenario would be believable. Maybe they just couldn't remember the numbers right. These men would have never passed Mr. Sims's tool test, not a chance. Was someone supposed to write the numbers down, and forgot to do it—I think it was the girl.

The girl with the Hello Kitty backpack, nobody thought she could build block walls and lift heavy bags of cement. Nobody would have guessed she would be empowered enough to provide her killers with a fake pin number. Mr. Sims taught some lessons. Some lessons have been learned, and some lost.

Daybook Journal: 2/23/99

I was watching a show last night about a guy who received a transplant operation. It was a hand. It was strange to see the guy with two differently colored and formed hands. Would he be more hesitant to bite his fingernails on the hand that didn't previously belong to him? Would it feel strange licking your fingers after eating a plate of ribs? The show didn't focus on that. He did learn the hand came from a man that had just been killed in a motorcycle accident in Paris. The man receiving the new hand, unknown by his doctors, had lost his hand in prison while operating an electric saw. Doctors were told, by the recipient, he had lost the hand in a construction accident.

Two men now connected. Would the motorcyclist have valued giving his hand to a man in prison? Does the prisoner deserve the hand? It might be useful having hands with different sets of fingerprints, especially since he reportedly was convicted of fraud. He later stole another patient's credit card and lifted cash from the hospitals transplant fund. He helped science, even though it was later reported the hand never really took and was eventually removed.

Daybook Journal: 11/14/99

One of our administrators died recently. He would give you the shirt off his back, even if it exposed the wear and tear of thirty years of overworking and under exercising. He has been greatly missed. They created a giant frog statue for him in the garden area that students pass daily as they enter the school. He loved frogs. I don't have any idea why. I mean Bullfrogs are treacherous. They will eat a medium sized bird perched and relaxing too closely to them; they will eat medium sized fish that aren't paying attention; they will even eat each other if they can fit their large Bullfrog mouths around a counterpart's body. At some point, nobody will remember him. That placard will continue to be plastered to the giant frog. It might give some friendless student standing near the garden, waiting to make a friend, something to read for a few of those awkward moments.

5

Loose Change

They just told me I would be at Colony.

Right, the new high school. That could be exciting. I hear a lot of other teachers have decided to move over there. You know—a change of pace.

Yeah, but I don't want to move all of my things over there! What a way to spend a summer…it's going to take me the whole time.

Well, at least it's a nice school.

All new media, new buildings—I mean once I get my stuff over there, it'll be great. But, they don't tell you how to get your stuff over there—they just say, 'You're at the new school'—and you go, 'Ok'. But I'm really thinking—son of a

bitch, I have to move a bunch of equipment.

I bet you can't pack all that equipment in a Corvette.

You're not kidding.

***

As I stood there shooting the breeze with the guy I have always referred to as the "Corvette Guy," because he drove a really nice Corvette, which is not a typical teacher car, I thought I am really happy I don't have to move anything this summer. He always seemed to park it in the administrators' parking lot—with a cover on it. Did that have something to do with them moving him to the new school? But, it was a nice car—I was jealous. I'm sure I wasn't the only one.

***

It was a long summer. Hot as hell. I imagined the Corvette Guy struggling to carry boxes with sweat running down his face and into his eyes as he tried to find a spot to set one of his many boxes down. Yet, I found it went far worse than I had thought. The guy with the red Corvette died of heart failure, according to a memo in one of the hundred emails I weeded through on that first day back. Poor bastard trying to reach his short rounded arms around a moving box pushed out an extra half foot by his belly. I never heard anything more about him. I'm not even sure he made it to moving day? I guess either way the year starts for the rest of us and we must move the work forward. I had my own issues to deal with.

I shared a room with a guy named Mr. Marin. He tried to be nice, but he would rather I get hurt and take some time off. I mean, he had nothing against me, but this was his last year, and make no mistake— this was his room. I rolled in a small file cabinet, and carried everything else in on my back—my rolling file cabinet was my classroom.

Como esta, Mr. Marin.

How are you? Come on in!

He spoke Spanish, but he would never respond to me in his Spanish. I think it was because I'm a white guy with an accent that sounds like I'm trying to mock the language.

He taught American Literature. He had been at this school for the past few decades. I talked to a few of his former students—they all praised his knowledge and cherished his influence. It was clear his heyday was behind him. He just wanted to get through the year and go take care of his sick sister out in Arizona. In the meantime, the administration has him sharing a room with some young punk with a pushcart, and they have him teaching 9th grade English for the first time in twenty years—what a send off.

I tended to stand outside of the classroom until Marin made his way out of the room and over to the teachers' lounge. It gets me out of his way, but also allows me to catch up with one of his former students, who teaches in the portable classroom next door.

***

Hey, Mr. Armendarez how are things going with Mr. Marin?

Good, he's a nice guy. He pretends he doesn't have a problem with me being there. Beyond that we have a great relationship.

He was my teacher.

Right—I heard he was a great teacher.

He was my 11th grade English teacher. I remember we read *The Joy Luck Club*—really he read it to us—he had a melodic voice. He was a great reader. Anyway, I was a good student—I was in the top 15 in my class, and you're supposed to get to be a part of the Daisy Chain. They pass out daisies at graduation. It's a big honor. I had just come from Mexico. We didn't have much money. I don't know if he knew anything about that, but he took me out shopping one day. He bought me a tie, a new shirt, and some new pants—he even bought me a new coat—the only thing he didn't buy me was shoes. It's funny because, just like now, he always wore slacks, a tie and a button up shirt to work, but he always wears old shoes.

Except for Friday—he wears those Caesar Chavez sandals.

Yeah, right. I guess you can wear sandals your last year. Nobody ever knew about what he did for me. I've tried to have dinner with him this year, but we can't seem to work it out. I think he's just done, and wants to get to the end of the year.

He doesn't look like he's in top shape. He looks sick—his hands shake.

I know—it's probably been a long time coming. Maybe Vietnam is finally catching up with him?

***

Sometimes in the spring, there's wind and a frost that lingers in the quad of the school as you take the long walk from the parking lot to the classroom. I know that Marin has a class, but I need to get in there to get my notes. The door creaks, but only one student in the class turns his head away from Mr. Marin. Marin's eyes are opened wide. His face is intense as he continues, "...he came out of his truck, and the door slammed shut—it was louder than he thought it would be. He was frightened. He was, for a moment pale, and ghost like. Then he caught himself—and even though he knew it was he that had shut the door, he could not ignore the lingering fear that it had caused him. It was a fear that he had tried to ignore, but it would return—like a fog that would follow him to the ends of his days.' That is how Gilman's character felt when she first peered into the yellow wallpaper. Gilman's character and Sgt. Johnson are the same in their first responses. There is a sense of surprise, a sense of shock, and then you draw conclusions and you make decisions—one decides to go crazy. One decides to continue to battle, moment by moment...unceasingly..."

I wouldn't mind staying to hear the rest of the lecture, but I already know Gilman's character ends up going mad and becoming one with the yellow wallpaper. It takes her a while, but the longer her husband keeps her locked in a room away from her loved ones—so that she might rest, and heal—the crazier she becomes. I wonder if it had been a portable classroom, rather than a countryside estate—she might have had very little to become one with. Beige walls with nothing on them, dust, and a cabinet filled with old junk and trash...those objects are hard to become one with.

***

As I walk to the class near the end of our thirty minute lunch, I hope I won't disrupt Mr. Marin. As usual, I carefully and slowly open the metal door. Light floods in briefly like a sudden pinhole blasted into a closed shoebox. The air is stale and thick. A tremendous collection of dust particles slowly dance in the small tunnel of light. At first, it seems I'm alone, but I spot Marin on his desk in the fetal position. He breathes, snoring lightly. Any major disruption might unbalance him forcing him to come crashing down on the dirty carpet—there would be no cushioning his fall. I walk out as carefully as I came in.

***

As the school year went by—nothing much happened. It's like when you ask your kids what happened at school when they get home. Sometimes, probably most of the time, they're telling the truth when they say "nothing." The seasons changed as much as they can for Southern California, and we influenced some kids to read a little more, and write something with just a little more meaning.

Summer has started, but it seems more like a spring afternoon. A mild wind blows through the trees in the senior quad. It is calm. I stand in front of my room before going to the office to turn in my keys. I see Mr. Marin, walking with his worn and tattered brief case—not a stylish leather one, but one of those old square ones, covered in what looks like a vinyl derivative, with the two clasping locks, the tiny combination wheels next to the handle. I spot him walking in the distance…too far away to say goodbye. There's nobody else in sight. He continues to walk toward the gate of the school without interruption. Finally, he disappears beyond the gate; he fades from the grass beyond—and I never see him again.

The room is mine now. I pull open a desk drawer. It was clogged and stuck closed. Paper peeked out at unorganized angles. Little was salvageable. At the bottom of one of the larger drawers I found his college diploma. Most of his junk went directly in the trash, but I set this aside, along with other assorted awards, certificates, and personal effects. I placed these bygones into an old box and I gave it to one of the older, more sensitive staff members to keep for him—even so, he never returned for any of it.

***

A year or two had passed. I asked one of my colleagues what had become of Mr. Marin. "Oh, he died a few months ago—he was out in Arizona taking care of his sister. Then he moved back to California and his health went south." I paused for some reflection. Then I rushed off to my room because my students were already there waiting for me. I tried to ignore the thought that we will all, at one time or another, walk alone through the front gate one last time. Even so, it would be nice to be remembered fondly.

Daybook Journal: 2/6/99

My son wanted to play baseball out front. How many times can he swing and miss before he gets tired enough for me to go in and take a nap?

Daybook Journal: 2/7/99

I went running and it felt horrible—I'm not going to do that again.

Daybook Journal: 2/8/99

My wife is taking a nap and my son is trying to ride his bike. He has a big helmet. We just got done reading *When I get Bigger*. It seems like he's already bigger. Sometimes it seems like he will be little forever—usually when he's screaming—and other times he seems big already. He can catch a football—sometimes—and he can ask good questions. Today he asked me if I built our house. I'm not sure why—he's never seen me build anything.

6

The Metamorphosis of Sisyphus

What does he mean when he says, 'Road less Travelled'? I mean, how would he know it's less traveled just because it's less worn…maybe the travelers were careful not to leave a mark.

Maybe Daniel, good question.

Daniel sat back a little in his seat, but Mr. A knew another question would be asked—it would not take long. It might be a good question—or a ridiculous question, but a question would be asked. And, it might be….

Mr. A, what is the deal with the road everyone traveled? I mean how long has that road been there….maybe…

Daniel, it's a metaphor. There's no road.

Well, Mr. A, there is a road, maybe not the same road—maybe even an alley?

Daniel, I don't think it's an alley—in fact—

This is where the lesson for the day had lost all of its meaning, and one simply waits for the bell to ring. Please let the bell ring.

Thank goodness.

See you Mr. A.

See you Daniel.

Nobody else says goodbye today, and nobody else asks a question today.

*

Today we are looking at an excerpt of *The Metamorphosis*, by Franz Kafka—

The cover makes it look like it's going to be about a guy trapped in a room—that looks like a small room...I would hate to be in that room!

Yes, Daniel that is a small room—just like the other day, it's a metaphor for what the character, and the author, are experiencing. As you can see, class, the cover of the book features the art work of Max Beckman, where we see a single character in the center of a very small room. How do you think this character feels?

Joey's hand shoots up, but Daniel intercedes.

He feels like he can't move—it's like if he wanted to get up he would just turn around in a circle and sit right back down—

—Daniel, Joey had his hand up. Joey, what do you think about the picture?

It's like being in this class. There's no escape.

That's exactly what it's like. Thank you Joey.

But there is much more room in this class. I mean if I want to go over to sharpen my pencil...I could move without anybody being in my way, right? What do you think Mr. A?

Daniel, I think Joey is speaking metaphorically and literally, but not in the way you're suggesting. Let's read.

Calm sets over the class. Most students hate to read, but they know even as Mr. A tries to mix it up and call on different students—somehow Daniel will find a way to do half of the reading. And to be fair, Mr. A will let him. Most of these kids can barely read, and it's like sticking a rusty needle in your eye to sit there and listen to them. When it happens, and it happens frequently, you have to agree with Joey, "There is [seemingly] no escape."

*

Get some paper out—let's write a story today.

Students very slowly get a piece of paper out. Some of them will get their paper out, but for some reason most of them will wait to be asked to also take out a pen or pencil.

Most students have a pen out. It's obviously going to be a good day. Daniel has questions.

What are we writing about today?

Everyone think of a setting in your head…. Now, I'm giving you exactly one minute to describe your setting. No detail is off limits. But, don't stop writing until I say to stop—even if you think you have nothing more to say. Ready—Go!

What if I want to change my setting later?

Daniel, you should be writing now.

But what if my setting is a place nobody would understand, like in the future?

I'm not going to respond to you until we're done. Stop talking and start writing!

I can't think of anything else.

Just keep writing Elsa.

………Time!

Mr. A notes that most students look exhausted, like they just took a three mile run. Today's youth, what have they become? When you're fourteen and obese and you get winded after a minute of freewriting, that should be a red flag. You should be extremely worried about your health.

Elsa, you look tired.

My arm hurts Mr. A.

My face hurts because I have to keep telling you to be quiet and write.

My arm hurts too, but you just have to play through the pain, right Mr. A.

That's right Daniel. Ok, let's think of a character. Think of a name, an age, a personality, a look…think of everything about them you can. You have two minutes to write about this character. Go!

Most students begin to write. Yet, Daniel has some questions.

Mr. A, what if my character is hard to understand; he's a character in the future.

Mr. A raises his index finger to his lips. Daniel is subdued for a few moments.

Mr. A, what do you think a guy with no eyes would be named?

Mr. A raises his index finger to his lips. Daniel is not subdued.

I mean he is a guy, sort of human, but he sees physically.
…..Time!

This time create a conflict—in fact, make sure you create an internal conflict and an external conflict.

What's the difference Mr. A?

Well Daniel, let's say you go out to lunch, after this class, and you ask a girl to Prom. But, she says no because she has a boyfriend—

Or, she sees that giant red birthmark on your face and thinks you don't take a shower.

Leo, go sit by Elsa—that's why you don't have a girlfriend and nobody likes you—think about that over in the back. Like I was saying, you would feel angry or sad, that would be internal. On the other hand, if you decide to punch Leo in the face at lunch, that would be external conflict. ...Ok, go—you have three minutes.

It's rare that Mr. A asks Daniel a question, but a story about a place unknown, with a character that communicates physically—Mr. A wondered what type of conflict a character of that sort would face.

.....Time.

Daniel, what's going on with your character?

He... if I can use gender to describe him—he is actually not man or women—is trying to impress his friend, who he loves, by psychically running as fast as he can. It's like running a sprint as fast as you can, but in your head. Like if you could play *Jenga* in your head, but do it really fast—that would be like psychic racing.

So, his friend can see him doing this?

That's the internal conflict—his friend could see, psychically, but she, if you have to use gender, is not really paying attention—and he can't keep it up forever.

Nice idea Daniel.

*

The cycle of the next day brings Mr. A and the class back to the exact same spot.

Why are the desks in a circle Mr. A?

It's a metaphor—you will see. Today we're going to talk about Sisyphus.

Who is Sisyphus, Mr. A?

Sisyphus is a guy who was cursed by the gods…

Why was he cursed by the gods?

He was cursed by the gods because he asked so many questions that nobody else could talk.

Daniel begins to open his mouth, and hesitates.

I'm just kidding Daniel; he wasn't cursed for asking questions. He was cursed for chronic deceitfulness.

What kind of chronic Mr. A?!

Slow down Leo.

The students begin to read around the circle, but somehow—the students read, Daniel reads, Elsa contributes, Daniel reads and others read as well.

You see, Sisyphus is a metaphor. It's a metaphor for the cycle of life and the options we have within that cycle. Like our daily lives, the sun sleeps in the East, dies to us, and is born again with the same magnitude in the West. We tend to live the same cycles daily and end up right in the same spot the next day…like the sun. We are reborn to live the same cycle.

I don't follow.

Daniel, you see, Sisyphus is cursed to push the boulder up the hill for eternity, but he decides to push it up, in every moment, with all of his effort and might.

Why bother?

Well Elsa, he cherishes each sensory experience, each moment—he loves the elements of life.

I would kill myself.

I don't think he can, but that's one option for us; many have argued that if life is truly absurd—that's a question worth asking....It's not easy being an absurd hero. You see Sisyphus knows his existence is absurd, but in spite of that he faces each absurd moment of his existence like a hero—without fear and with a sense of duty.

What's his duty if the ball rolls down and his efforts never accomplish anything?

Daniel, I don't know for sure; maybe the duty is to him alone? What is it? Maybe it has something to do with his self-worth or pride. I can't say for sure?

Daniel pauses, possibly to contemplate, and decides not to ask another question.

***

Mr. A did not see or hear from Daniel for some time. In fact, at the semester Daniel was transferred out of Mr. A's class, and aside from some cross campus sightings at a passing period or at lunch, he didn't speak to Daniel or answer anymore of his questions.

***

I hate these meetings. I hope nobody asks any questions to slow this thing down. We'll be here forever if they let Ms. Johnson start asking questions.

Once you let her get started she just won't stop. Did you have that Daniel kid from a few years ago—the kid would ask a question every few seconds—it drove me crazy.

Was he the kid with the red patch on his forehead?

Yeah, that's the kid. He's probably asking someone questions right now. I'm glad he's not at this meeting.

I don't think he is asking anyone any questions. I think he died of an asthma attack last year. That's what one of the office ladies told me.

That's horrible! …maybe there was a reason he had so many questions to ask? Of course, he never really agreed with any of my answers. I'm not sure why he kept asking.

The meeting continued well past its scheduled end time. Ms. Johnson asked several questions. None of them mattered much, and none of the answers seemed to satisfy her. Yet she continued, and continued, and she continued. Mr. A learned nothing at this meeting—and neither did anyone else. He hoped Daniel's questions eventually led to some useful answers.

Daybook Journal: 2/4/99

I'm at lunch, at work—there's a baby shower after work. I won't be making it to that. We're having an ongoing chat about people who breast feed kids that are old enough to walk, kids that can crawl up and unbutton mom's blouse like it's a fridge.

Daybook Journal: 2/12/99

Some kid read a TV guide for our free reading time. I wonder if he has his whole week planned out for his TV viewing. He was probably being more productive with his time than any of us.

Daybook Journal: 5/22/99

It's cold as hell today. Some kids stole my jacket!!

7

Time Out for Literacy

The first day of class sets the tone. Sixth grade. It may have been fun as a kid, but as a teacher—it's not as joy filled. A chubby Mexican kid shouts out, "Mr. A…is that your name? Mr. A!" Laughing forcefully, his chin jiggling slightly. "Let's have a seat guys." A late kid strolls in. "Why are you late?" He sits down with a wide smile. "That's Juan, Mr. A.," the chubby kid says as he bends his plastic ruler back and forth; he shifts to loosen up his undershirt, which he is wearing as though it weren't an undershirt, but an outer shirt, which is much too snug. "Take out your Life Skill book."

Reluctantly, the books appear. "Can I read Mr. A," asks the chubby kid. "Sure," I reply. His words come with more clarity than I expect. He doesn't stop at the first paragraph—he continues for a full page. "Popcorn Mr. A?" asks the fat kid. "Popcorn, good idea." Everyone slumps in their seats and looks away, as though they can't be seen if they don't look up or make eye contact. "Popcorn!! Juan!!" yells the chubby kid. "Ooooooh" the class replies.

Juan hesitates. He looks at the page. Then he looks to his left. Then he looks at the page. "The hetylif is the bstlif to ssttaarr…" I have to put a stop to this immediately! Not so much for him, but for me and every one of the other kids in the class. This is torture. This is water boarding. I have to close Guantanamo immediately. Most teachers would give him time to try. Don't shut him down; give him a chance. No way! This turns out the same every time. Every person in the class is in agony; the kid reading is in agony. Well, maybe he's getting warmed up. Maybe he will improve if you give him some practice! Not on my watch. "Good Juan: 'The healthy life is the best life to start'—that's great." "I will read," says a skinny girl in the back. "Great." "That's Maria, Mr. A" says the chubby kid.

Maria has saved us all. She reads beautifully. Then the chubby kid reads beautifully. Then Maria—then the fat kid. Thirty minutes elapses and we get to the questions. The first part of the first day is nearly over—and after break these kids rotate to their next teacher.

The bell sounds, and we're all released. Ms. Kinny sees me and we walk up to the staff room. "Did you have Juan? He is such a sweet kid. You know he can't read. He needs lots of extra help" says Ms. Kinny. "He seems nice enough, but the heavy kid seems like a solid student— I'd like to find out what he's interested in." Ms. Kinny replies, "Future interests!? Welcome to the Sans. These kids don't have future interests. They might want to buy some Mexican candy or some chips right after they get out of school. Most of them are not thinking very far ahead. But, a kid like Juan—he needs to learn how to read. He's such a sweet kid. Did you see the smile on that kid?"

The staff room is an empty box with three mismatched tables and a mixed lot of chairs, some of which are kid-sized. Ms. Wartz walks in. She's the principle—if she sat on one of the kid chairs, her ass would swallow it up like a sink hole. There's a lot of room in there. I know it sounds insensitive and catty, but she is one of the worst people I have ever met. I have, in short time, surmised that Mr. Sims has slipped right up there and claimed land. He has constructed a small village there. It's sickening. Mr. Sims is a comedian. He tests his jokes out on us over the next few weeks in the staff room. I have heard his whole set five or six times. "Maria can you sharpen your eye pencil and put your name on your paper....then I turned around in my cardigan and wrote on the board, waiting for Maria to stab me in the back with her eyeliner pencil." I just can't laugh at that. I feel sort of bad—maybe I'm just not his audience.

"Mr. A, you have Juan, right? I've been working with him on his reading" says Mr. Sims. "I do have that kid—big smile. ...That fat kid is real sharp. His math and science is the best in the class." Mr. Sims replies, "I don't think I remember that kid? But I do remember Maria...every time I turn my back to her I think my goodness we have to write a paragraph right away to dull that eye pencil before she shanks me in the back!" "Right, smart—good defense starts with good offense Mr. Sims," I suggest.

That next week I see the chubby kid running as fast as he can on the grass field. "Pasale, pasale!" He gets a clean pass. He takes a hard shot at the goal. "GOOOAAALLL!" That's a big fat smile.

"Guys, what do you think about starting a soccer tournament?" "What do you mean, Mr. A?" I explain, "Let's organize teams of five and get ten teams in a bracket. I'll get some trophies for the winning team. Take this sheet. Go see if you can sign up some teams." "Where's Juan? Let's get him to help," one kid suggests. "No, he's with Ms. Kinny—she's working with him," replies Fredo—the chubby kid's sidekick. Then he follows his comment with his best dick sucking face—several thrusts of his tongue into his cheek while jigging his right hand back and forth as one might eat a Popsicle at supersonic speed. He thought he was very funny, and so did the rest of the kids. I tried to erase the image from my mind, and shift the focus back to the tournament.

The next day the kids were excited for the soccer tournament. "Let's go guys. You have twenty minutes and then we call time."

"Pasale, pasale….mono, mono…" They run their hearts out. They run the entire lunch. How does that kid stay chubby? He must be on a strict and faithful diet of Mexican candy and Hot Cheetos. That kid can move. "GOOAALL!" He runs in a baby circle and falls to the grass making a snow angel formation…with that big fat smile. At nearly the same time Ms. Kinny exits her class with Juan. He has a smile on his face. I know Ms. Kinny is putting all she has into that kid's education. She once said in the teacher's lounge, "Teachers wouldn't seem marginal if there were more parents in the world." She's working to fill that gap.

But, let's face it, I'm pretty marginal. I'm raising a family, going to school full-time, and trying to put myself in a position to get a college job. A day laborer could come in and tell them to turn to page 12 and answer the questions at the end of the chapter. And, it would be better understood because he would be explaining it in a language they would all understand. But, he couldn't teach Juan to read—can anyone?

Of course, how would a day laborer respond to some of these kids? "Sophie can you turn to page 10?" "Fuck this shit." "Sophie, go to the office." "This is shit; they aren't going to do anything!" She was right—she's a super fat girl that looks twenty-five years old. She's thirteen. She hates the world. Who can blame here. She's fat, illiterate, and her parents are in a gang. Good luck with that. Teachers are what are broken in this system? What about the day Fredo snapped when I asked him for the tenth time to sit back down in his seat? I don't even know where he was headed, and I'm pretty sure he didn't know either. He just wanted out. If he gets out of his seat he's one step closer to escape, one step further from total confinement.

"What did you say—get out of my seat!? I'm sharpening my pencil!"

"But we're trying to read. You need to learn when it's ok to get up and sharpen your pencil! Can we read when you're over there sharpening your pencil? We are all distracted when you stop to joke with

Maria...and then everyone stops to look at Maria—and Maria pretends to laugh even though you're not funny."

Maria likes him and would laugh at anything he did, even though he's disgusting and doesn't shower, or groom, or finish his food before he starts talking, or wears enough deodorant not to stink. The cheap cologne shower he took after playing soccer must have been enough to get it done. Maria is bound to pick a solid life partner and father for her children.

Fredo sits back down for a moment. Then he yells "AAHHH" as he grabs the weeding sickle—that's on the shelf for the gardening club. He runs toward the wall and with full force he swings the weeding sickle into the wall. The sickle sticks into the wall of our portable class. He lets go of it and looks at me. Luckily, and he wouldn't have known this, I grew up with a crazy mom who would throw a speaker or an entire stereo across a room when she freaked out every now and again—so I'm unimpressed with his exhibition of crazy town. I have been to crazy town. I grew up in crazy town. He's surprised with my lack of reaction, yet I do note this sort of thing should never be allowed in a classroom. This wouldn't happen in a middle class school. Parents would revolt—it would be outlandish. But not here. This place was up the Nung River, about four clicks past the last checkpoint.

I send him to the office. I do the paperwork: *Fredo got up out of his seat and with all of his might he stabbed a gardening sickle into the wall of the portable. This behavior is unacceptable in a classroom.* I send it up with another student, but Fredo comes back to class about fifteen minutes later. What do you mean Fredo comes back about fifteen minutes later? Do you mean to say you can get up out of your seat in a California classroom and stab a gardening sickle into a wall with all of your might, and yell "AAHHH" as you do it—and absolutely nothing happens to you?!

The Vice Principle of Discipline is the type of lady you would picture living in a clean, yet antique mobile home. She would have all of her

Hummels lined up neatly on the top of a particle board shelf. She would have a water color of a clown hanging upon her panel board covered living room wall. It would be dusty where dust collects in spots that are hard to get to, and the carpet would appear clean even though it would be original, bacteria filled from things that just happen in a mobile home over the course of time. A spilled cup of coffee that had been rigorously scrubbed, a tipped over piece of lemon meringue pie that slid off her nephew's tiny Styrofoam plate—those plates can be tricky—or the known and unknown spots where her former cat had puked, phlegm coughed, peed, and/or squirted out some diarrhea while jumping upon the corner of the couch in its twilight months.

Her hands look as though they're encased with the translucent skin they use to wrap sausages. She holds her coffee cup like a heavy paper weight. It dips forward and she squeezes the ceramic handle—as though it might slip from her plump fingers at any moment. She takes great effort to lift it to her lips. The liquid is brown from thick cream that flows into her mouth like hot gravy.

I think she must not have read the referral I sent up to the office. She must have been out of the office, or in the middle of an important task. *Please allow me to explain again what Fredo did. He took a garden sickle, a sharp metal implement, which could be considered a weapon, and he blasted it into a wall. This seems to me to be a serious safety issue. Surely you did not read my referral, or I did not explain the situation in enough detail. He defied my authority several times when I had asked him to sit down, and then he endangered the entire classroom, or at least the students sitting near the area where he swung the sharp object into the wall. I am glad he did not swing the implement into another student! Please do not send him back to class!!*

She doesn't send him back to class this time. She would later explain to me these students just need love and kindness. Fredo is a good kid. She had a good talk with him. She feels like he's going to be much better now. But if he is not, maybe I need to get him more involved in the activity of the classroom.

After the soccer tournament ends we make up a handball tournament. This time it's teams of three, with a single elimination bracket. I figure some of these kids might end up in the system, and handball is not the worst skill one can have. Sociological studies would suggest my attitude is predetermining my expectations of them, thus their expectations of themselves. You're right—let's assume they're all going to college, and set them up in college prep classes. Then when their parents influence them to drop out and start working for the family, I'm sure they can get a job doing algebra problems and writing five paragraph essays. They'll be loaded with resume building skills. Knowing some plumbing, and some auto, and some carpentry wouldn't serve them at all—it would only limit their futures. How will they get into a state college?! I went to a state college and look how successful I am!

In fact, I seem so successful that little Consuelo's dad asked if he might be able to bring little Consuelo over to my house to see what valuable prizes he might earn if he works hard and stays in school. Apparently little Consuelo had not been pulling his weight in school or at home. So, he and his dad pull up to my house one night. House is too strong a description. We live in a one bedroom box with a shared front yard that overlooks some apartments where gang guys are always sitting outside drinking beer. Little Consuelo's dad comes in and sits down with his son. He says, "Consuelo, if you work hard—this could be your life." Really?! Up to that point I had tried hard not to reflect, but little Consuelo's dad made me want to kill myself. Consuelo must be thinking—"Are you kidding dad?! This is it? So, if I work hard I can live in a tiny one bedroom with my two year old son, and I can sleep on a sofa sleeper. Yes, work hard and stay in school. If you want to live in a normal house, in a normal neighborhood, don't become a teacher. I wonder why our more educated are not becoming teachers.

"Mr. A did you bring your balls?" the chubby kids asks with a grin.

"Of course I brought my balls. Are you ready to do this?" I hand the tiny blue ball to the chubby kid and he gives me his giant smile. "Who's on your team?" "Well, Juan is doing his reading, so I'm going to play with Fredo," he says. The chubby kid gets in position and he tosses the ball up while he swings his fat arm around and cracks the ball with his mitt sized hand. "Ven...Pegar...pagar!" And on and on it goes. And, no cologne shower will make them smell better. They laugh and they sweat, and they smile. The bell rings. We will play the quarter finals on Tuesday. As we walk, Juan exits the ramp of Ms. Kinny's room. I don't know if his reading will ever improve, but he has a mother in Ms. Kinny and we should all be so lucky to have a mother that wants us to succeed.

I no longer work in the Sans. For a short while I meet with my former colleagues for some lunch or a get together. I get the updates.

"Mr. Rossen died!"

"He was young, right. Wasn't he in his thirties!?" I ask. "I think he was. But he just up and died. It was very sad. I don't know if he had much of a family or not, but it was terrible." The Sans is a dangerous place. You aren't overly surprised when a kid dies, but the teachers are supposed to stay alive until they retire, and then of course die almost immediately—just as the pension math wizards have prophesied. In the Sans you don't want to walk around the streets without some friends, and even then you're a target. In the day, most of the time you're ok, but don't be out for any reason at night. One of the initiations to join one of the gangs is to stab someone. Not necessarily to death, but who wants to take the chance. One of my former students, let's call him Jose, was in a gang, and he was very quiet, soft spoken, and polite. I knew he was a gang kid. He didn't do much work, but he understood the idea of respect for one's domain.

I had his brother a few years later, and one day he came in and said, "Jose is dead—they shot him."

Why did they shoot him? I don't know? Initiation? They shot one of their guys, so they had to shoot one of those guys? There is some logic in it—I mean mathematically. At least until a baby gets blasted in the crossfire. The thing I don't understand is why the "better" parents don't just up and move. There were some "better" parents—but how good could they have been to allow their kids to grow up in that environment? Does it make you mad to hear that? Am I talking about you?

Juan's story ends in similar fashion. Juan wouldn't back down. He said something. Something was said back. They killed him. From what I hear, they shot him right in the face, so his mom couldn't have an open casket. They printed up t-shirts and had a car wash. They put him in the ground. People said, "He was a good kid. A good sweet kid. He could have done better. Ms. Kinney put so much time and effort into him. He was really getting it. It's just really too bad."

Years later, I was having lunch at a Marie Callender's Restaurant with my son, who was now in high school, and I ran into one of those giving teachers of the Sans. She was as steady and as kind as ever—hair a little disheveled...like it always had been.

"Well, I hope that some of those kids made it past the gangs," I inquired. "Oh, I know they did—now that I'm old I go to all of the high school graduations. It's great to see some of them grown up—walking up to get their diplomas. It really makes you feel good for them," she replied.

"I wonder how some of them are doing—I can't remember his name—short chubby kid—he loved science, and he was really good at soccer, and he was faster than you would expect. He would have had another year after I left. I know I'm probably describing a dozen different kids."

"No, I think I know who you're talking about—I think he is doing ok—I think he came by the school not too long ago."

"It was great talking to you. Tell whoever is left I said hello."

At work, at my current teaching job, I keep all of my yearbooks in a stack on my book shelf. I dust them off once a year, but I typically don't read them. I want to make sure I have something to do for a few weeks after I retire. After seeing my old friend I couldn't resist. You don't see any negative when you pick the paper yearbook up and remember kids that you had long forgotten—kids that you would never have thought of again if you had not picked up that yearbook. In the pictures they are all behaving perfectly. None of them look like they would cause any trouble. And most of them wouldn't, and most of them never did.

Have fun Mr. A,

Hope you could forgive me for being really bad in your class, but hey I'm the classes clown. Ooh And Happy 29th old birthday. Man are you old (just kidding). Well congratulations and remember me, but don't member the other people. Well bye. See ya next year.

Love, Stranger

P.S.—Remember north, Remember south, Remember me and my big mouth. But don't forget me!

What makes a kid join a gang? Not enough hugs? I've had some miserable times; why didn't I join a gang? What do gangs really offer? Warmth? I've lived in some cold environments; I might have joined a gang if one had offered me a warm cup of cocoa and a comfortable pillow to sit on next to a fire. When it's cold every day, and it smells like cold, and the snow crunches under your boots, and your feet feel like they have never been warm, you will do almost anything to get warm. There were times I would just hang out in the bus stop, yet someone would open the door, and then someone else would open the door, and then someone else would open the door. Being warm a little became a reminder that you would be cold again very soon.

My house wasn't even warm. The tiny heater only reminded you of the warm you once felt. We were so poor we didn't have expensive gloves. At best it was a hug enveloped by damp cotton mittens. Surely, I was almost cold enough to join a gang.

8

Marshall High School

The metal detectors don't seem to be working. It's a big place, too big to be monitored. How does that make you feel? Do you have a kid in school here...somewhere?

He must have walked right in...through a side door. "We are on lock down! I repeat—we are on lockdown! Please don't let your students out and lock the door!" ...and again and again... We thought nothing of it. Business as usual. There's a lock down here and a lock down there...every other week, and what? Do we panic now—this time or next time?

I have a lesson to teach...10th grade English...I'm a student teacher...lock down or not, I need to get through this lesson, get out of this school and get a real job before my newborn son realizes I'm a loser. Today we're going to cover, no matter what happens, why that guy in *The Pearl* was duped into selling that very pricy pearl for much less than it was worth...was it cultural capital, lack of representation, or too much excitement? Can you place a price upon what he ended up paying? We shall see.

Ms. Mary picks up a call from the office. She crouches in the corner on the phone…what a freak…big awkward lady is probably going to tell my student-teaching advisor to give me a bad grade. She won't ruin my lesson with her crouching! I shift my focus and turn to address the class.

So then, what would you have done if you had found this pearl?

I would have moved to a different village and sold it to some other guys.

Good idea! We'll see that he does try to do something like that, but I'm not sure he would have found anyone else, that was honest, that easily—that would not have tried to take advantage of him. They wanted to get that pearl and make some riches.

I would have taken it to the swap meet!

These kids love the swap meet. There are few other places you can buy some chickens, a wrench and a mango on a stick. Ms. Mary gets another call. What's going on? She won't sabotage me! She is back to her crouching again. What is her deal? She's trying to steal my thunder! She's trying to ruin my life.

What's the point here? Are all people evil, or are these folks simply a product of some sort of village capitalism?

Oh, people are evil—they will shoot you for just standing there to get a pencil out of your locker.

Yeah, you can look at them wrong, or step on their new shoe and they will hit you up.

So then, you don't see this as odd or wrong these guys were trying to get this guy's pearl on the cheap…I mean he found this thing, but he isn't the one that's going to get rich…some other guy was trying to get rich…and this guy did all the work!

That's the white people!

Yeah, I bet the guy buying the pearl was a white guy…you can't get a head…the white guys control everything!

Well, actually the guy trying to buy the pearl was not white…does that make you start to question human nature in general—or is this just one group of bad guys he has run into…is it a matter of the wrong village at the wrong time?

It's like when I was at the King Taco, and I was just sitting there, and this cop comes up to me…this is my King Taco…and he says how long have you been here…and I'm just eating a burrito.

I don't follow your point.

King Taco is the bomb, and I just want to sit there and eat a burrito—that's my point.

There Ms. Mary goes again! That's like the sixth call. She is crouching again—all crazy. What is her problem?

Flap, flap, flap, flap—(helicopter sounds)—

What's that!—a helicopter?

Yeah, wait—that might be two helicopters?

I know you guys want to look outside, but we're on lock down.

Students fidget in this windowless portable classroom. The thin walls vibrate a little when the helicopter makes its pass.

Flap, flap, flap, flap…

We know it might be serious when we hear the helicopters directly overhead. They usually don't have them directly overhead.

What's going on?

I heard two kids were shot in the "A" building.

Shot in the "A" building?

Oh, yeah, I was at the end of the hall…some kids were shot.

Who did it?

I didn't see them, but I heard it was gang retaliation.

Gangs—did they get them?

No, they hit two other kids—that's what they were saying. They hit a girl in the arm and some guy in the leg—I think?

Do these guys not take shooting lessons?

Everyone was running.

Shot a kid!? Are you sure?

Yeah, I was up there. All the kids were running down the stairs, falling down, and pushing each other.

It was two girls that got shot.

No, it was some gangster—shot in the face…rat, tat, tat, tat!

I heard he missed the guy and shot some other people…some girl and a guy that was at his locker.

Ok, we don't know what is going on—let's stay with this guy and his pearl. Follow me on page 12. Let's evaluate what's going on here. This is a desperate place …or at least it can be…Steinbeck says, *On the beach the hungry dogs and the hungry pigs of the town searched endlessly for any dead fish or seas bird that might have floated in on a rising tide.* There are lots of kind people in this village, and lots of families, but this is a place where it's not uncommon to be on the lookout to take an advantage over your situation, whether…it's originally yours or not…this is an example of foreshadowing…..he goes on to say …*the whole Gulf so that all sights were unreal and vision could not be trusted…* In other words, things are not always as they seem.

That sounds familiar…I'm always looking to roll up on something.

If you ever roll up on something of mine I am going to beat you.

Roll up means steal, Mr. A.

Yeah, I know what roll up on means. These people just want to get lucky…they're desperate for luck. Steinbeck says, *But the pearls were accidents, and the finding of one was luck, a little pat on the back by God or the gods or both.* Yet, most of the people were humble, and had a true sense of honor. And then Kino found a shell…and he was so excited. But just like when you find a $20 bill on the ground…you have to look twice to make sure you saw what you thought you saw. The book says, *In this Gulf of uncertain light there were more illusions than realities.* But then he gets it open and *It was the greatest pearl in the world.* So, it's this giant pearl—these things are worth a ton of money. This is like finding a suitcase with a gold bar in it—

...or a suitcase of cocaine, right Mr. A.

Sort of, but it came from the ocean, and it belonged to nobody.

So no guy with a gun is going to be coming after you!

Right...those of you that read further know that sometimes when you have something of value—no matter where it came from, guys with guns come after you. And, you know what happened? *The news stirred up something infinitely black and evil in the town...* People started to think of what they could do if they had all that money the pearl would bring them. It was the power of a belief. A belief that if you can do "this thing" you can be someone or you might be important. Kino imagines him and his wife in fine clothing...do things usually work out as ideally as you imagine they might?

I'm not sure what 'ideally' means, but nothing I try ever works out.

That's because she is too pretty for you—ask out Maria instead. Ok, Maria won't go out with him either...right Maria?!

Maria smiles, but we can all see that she likes Jose. All the girls like Jose. It doesn't make any sense to me, but it makes clear sense to Maria.

Then Kino thought of a gun... *A rifle.* Guns bring great power, right? Do they? Kino thought it would. He wanted to be a man! Would this make him a man?

Guns never make anybody a man!

Shut up before I blast you! Ha, Ha, ha.

Steinbeck goes on to explain ...*by saying what his future was going to be like, he had created it. A plan is a real thing, and things projected are experienced. A plan once made and visualized becomes a reality along with other realities—never to be destroyed but easily to be attacked...* But, will this vision destroy him and his entire family? ...This belief...is it going to destroy them? Juana, Kino's wife, says, *This thing is evil...This pearl is like a sin! It will destroy us.*

Ms. Mary, with a smashed up crazy face, is on the phone again—I can't tell if that's her usual face or another new, yet very similar face. You should stay with a normal face. If you go with the crazy face all the time, on a daily, hourly, basis—than, you switch it to an altogether alternate crazy face, it makes it near impossible to interpret what the currently just as crazy face represents. But, It does sound like a sky of helicopters outside.

Flap, flap, **Flap**, flap...

Steinbeck tells us that *This was to be the day from which all other days would take their arrangement. Thus they would say, "It was two years before we sold the pearl," or, "It was six weeks after we sold the pearl."* This day would change everything for Kino and his family; just this one choice would change everything.

The noise from outside became louder, but luckily in this windowless portable—I can keep some of their focus. Nevertheless, the one senior in this class is doing a lot of fidgeting with his backpack, and the kid in the back just slipped into a full sleep.

Kino took so much care with this giant pearl. It was like his prized possession. It's like your special new knife... *The great pearl was wrapped in an old soft piece of deerskin and placed in a little leather bag, and the leather bag was in a pocket in Kino's shirt.* He couldn't wait to take it out...for that moment of anticipation—to take it out and trade it for what would be the rest of his life...

It makes me wonder how much time and effort went into our school shooter's preparations. Did he wrap the gun in something special, or did he just toss it in his pocket? Did he know those shots would be traded for what would become the rest of his life?

But Kino had grown tight and hard. He felt the creeping of fate, the circling of wolves, the hover of vultures. He felt the evil coagulating...and he was helpless.

Flap, flap, flap, flap—che, che, che...

Mr. A, those helicopters sound like they're going to land on the roof. What's going on out there?

The kid in the middle row was moving around like he has to take a piss. I want to tell him to relax, but if he does have to take a piss—what am I going to tell him…here's a trash can buddy…get busy.

So anyway, things are getting worse and worse. His wife said *Kino, this pearl is evil. Let us destroy it before it destroys us. Let us crush it between two stones. We will not be cheated. I am a man.* Is being a man worth being destroyed? It goes on to say, *He heard the rush, got his knife out and lunged at a dark figure and felt his knife go home, and then he was swept to his knees and swept again to the ground.* It turns out he killed this man! Now what can he do?

He is done! Better drive to Mexico, right Mr. A?

This is what his wife says—[she] *knew that the old life was gone forever. A dead man in the path and Kino's knife, dark bladed beside him…peace…now it was gone, and there was no retrieving it.*

More creeping—what the hell—and that kid won't stop with the restless moving and the backpack shuffling. That kid normally sits there without a word. Cool as hell. A senior in a sophomore class. Nice kid. Never gives anyone any problems. Looks like a trouble maker, but must have done some maturing since he was a sophomore. I need to keep this lesson moving before all is lost.

So this guy is in too deep now. Kino says *This pearl has become my soul…If I give it up I shall lose my soul.* Is this a sane belief? The only thing he really has is a belief. That's it. He has his family, love, and this belief.

Is it worth the violence and the death and destruction? Would you give up the belief, in Kino's case the belief he must get the money to be happy, to stop the violence and death and the destruction. He has the power to stop it…to put an end to it. It's that easy—but just like the Hatfield's and McCoy's, he just can't stop…and will it be his doom? One choice away from freedom or destruction.

Kino is never going to make it. He should go out like a hero and just start shooting fools.

Yeah, it says *Every escape is cut off.*

Good Juan—does that mean he can do nothing now—nothing for his family? It's like he's possessed with this belief. It says…*some animal thing was moving in him so that he was cautious and wary and dangerous; some ancient thing out of the past of his people was alive in him.*

His wife should take him out—he's destroying his family. He's not a man.

He's not your man, Maria. You would take his pearl and buy purses.

Shut up!

Is the pearl evil? Is he evil now? Steinbeck says *Kino thrusts the pearl back into his clothing, and the music of the pearl had become sinister in his ears and it was interwoven with the music of evil.*

I think he can change—everyone can change if they really want to change.

Keep believing that. Is your boyfriend going to change—no he's not.

Shut up!

Flap, Flap, Flap...bang, bang, rattle, rattle...

The creeping and crouching is continuous. Now there's an orchestra of movement in this windowless portable. Pages turning, feet shuffling, zippers zipping...

I can't hear over the helicopters. What's all the noise outside!?

Let us crack the door open Mr. A—just for a peek. You look out there and tell us what's going on.

Maybe in a few minutes. Let's get through the rest of this—we're almost done. It says *They were the trackers, they could follow the trail of a bighorn sheep in the stone mountains. They were as sensitive as hounds...Kino lay as rigid as a tree limb. He barely breathed...He knew these inland hunters...they managed to live because of their ability to hunt, and they were hunting him...Kino slowly drew his knife to his hand and made it ready. He knew what he must do...That was his only chance in the world...Kino was not breathing, but his back arched a little and the muscles of his arms and legs stood out with tension and a line of sweat formed on his upper lip...They would be circling...*

...Flap, Flap, Flap, Flap...

...and searching, peeping, and they would come back sooner or later to his covered track...The trackers would find his trail, he knew it. There was no escape, except in flight....And then helplessness and hopelessness swept over him, and his face went black and his eyes were sad.

Pound, pound, click, flap, flap.......flap...

... "Perhaps I should let them take me." You see what's happening here? This....

She was in a corner with her gigantic grotesque body turned away from the class. I am disturbed, yet I will not give her my focus. Some of the girls on that side of the room seem concerned and bewildered—which seems appropriate. She stands up suddenly. Almost instantly Ms. Mary gains the attention of the entire class.

That's enough Mr. A. Ok—everyone in the first row stand up and walk one at a time out of the room—ok, ...go now! Go! Go!...

The room is silent, and it looks like I will never finish my *Pearl* lesson. I don't know that these kids learned anything today.

Now, second row start walking out. –Go, now!

I look out the door and I see the police. Tons of police, and the helicopters circles in the air. The police are grabbing kids as they come out. They're running them away from the building. These kids have never been so obedient in their lives.

The class has emptied, and I peer outside. They have one of the kids off to the side—hands behind his back, bent over a police car. The teacher crouches behind the bookcase. She pulls out a backpack. "The gun must be in the back pack. I saw him throw it behind the book case when he got up to walk out the door." I stand there with a retard's face, and the clouds part completely, and suddenly I understand why she was crouching in the corner. She feared for her life. A killer in the classroom, and so on and so forth. I'm sure they got some laughs later in the teacher's lounge about that student teacher that kept the calm because he was more focused on Steinbeck's make believe world than the shooter four seats away from him, dead row center. I ended up getting a "B-" in student teaching. Which is the grade you give people to suggest to them, without the fear of being sued, that they should not go into teaching.

And like a *dead bundle* they zip tie his hands together and place him in the back of the police car. *And the music of the pearl drifted to a whisper and disappeared.* But, it was too late; the decision had been made long ago... *he had lost one world and had not gained another.....He was terrified of that monster...*and the monsters he would soon meet. And the monster he had become.

It's funny how differently you see the world when you're in high school. Even students that have been out for a year can look back with incredible hindsight when they think back to their former selves. They claim they will become fashion designers and Lamborghini owners and live in mansions with beautiful friends. I like their ambition, and I always wish them the best. But, usually when they come back to visit, or I see them out there in the world, they're working fools, just like the rest of us, struggling to pay bills, and looking forward to the next marginal goal that's sure to move them forward a little. Of course, some students don't have lofty goals.

I walked into the class the other day, after taking a between period bathroom break, and I walked in on a student doing push-ups. I thought, that's ambitious to get an extra work out in, when you can. I sort of wished I had the fortitude to jump down and hit a set of push-ups from time to time. I asked him what he was doing, and he said he was doing push-ups because he was practicing for prison. Do they have push up contests in prison? He said they didn't but that lots of the brothers are always doing push-ups.

In prison they're always doing push-ups? I thought being in a push-up position seems like the last position you want to be in if you're in prison. I wanted to express this to him, because I'm a teacher, and you need to teach to all students,…it seemed like a really bad idea to get on your hands and knees in prison, even if others first get down on their hands and knees and suggest that we should all have a push-up contest—seems like that could be a trick. You would think if you're going to practice anything to go to prison it would be how to stand in a corner in an impenetrable ball. Or you might want to work on your takedown defense, or frankly one might do some butt cheek work…not getting past a solid clench might be cause for embarrassment and frustration…they might just give up and walk away.

I didn't share any of these ideas with him.

My hope is that he doesn't go to prison. He claimed that all black guys go to prison, but I corrected him and I think he listened.

Daybook Journal: 8/13/01

After a 17 hour drive to Colorado we turned down the wrong street and got our truck stuck in the snow near the edge of someone's driveway. It was high in the hills and it was very dark. I tried to dig a trench with a small camping shovel under the rear tire. Every time I tried to attempt another escape from this icy driveway I feared our truck would roll back and down the driveway into the giant fancy house below. As I worked on the pointless ditch from time to time nearby residents drove by and took a look. I'm sure a few of them wondered how long it would take these ignorant people in their two wheel drive with California plates to dig themselves out. Finally I walked down the thirty yard stretch of driveway and asked if I might use their phone. They were reluctant and annoyed. I looked into their warm and cozy cabin, at these beautiful people. I hated them.

9

An Angry Old Man and Unfocused Rants of Death, Rebirth and Love

We study the theory of death and rebirth. It's an archetypal cycle. The primitives used it to form their religions. The argument is that your religion is created from what you hear and see in your society. The primitives had few formal philosophers, and even fewer stables of diverse thinkers within their limited populous. They looked out the window of their hut and saw trees, water, birds, a moon, and a sun. They noticed these objects existed as part of a larger cycle. The sun was born every morning and it died every night. Plants died; then near the same spot they came to life again. The snow came; it died away with the birth of a brighter sun. Some of them thought if they created death they would create life. So that's just what they did. They killed. They sacrificed. They built fire pits that became the giant mouths of these immeasurable gods—these various gods they surmised must be in control of these complex cycles of death and rebirth—and to please these gods, and to help generate the mechanics of the cycle they fed those mouths their extra babies, little brothers, kings, irritating wives, donkeys, and the like.

Of course, people eventually began to complain, so they leaned more towards killing baby goats, lambs, and eventually fatted calves. Yet, from time to time brave individuals would continue to sacrifice their own lives for the benefit and continued prosperity of the people. What is this idea of sacrificing one life for the many? It's a noble ideal. We hold them up as heroes—wasted lives for the better good. Is it something to be achieved, or sought after? Will not the villagers love me and remember me well if I sacrifice for them? The youth of ancient times have competed for the chance to be honored as a sacrifice for their kings, yet some have narrowly missed the mark and had to travel back to their villages in shame—and, to the disappointment of their families and friends. Sometimes one can give life through servitude, and this also constitutes a worthy sacrifice.

The girls in my classes are having babies. They are creating life, and creating death, of their own childhoods, dreams, and freedoms. Will this death create more life? Statistically it will. The short generational cycle approaches, and then it appears, and then it explodes—it dies creating new life. They are creating something they can love. But their dreams—more accurately their chances to live better than their parents, have been killed. Why are you so pessimistic? They can love their babies. They can still go to school. They can read books. They can become professionals. Some might, but most will become welfare recipients. Most have become marginalized. They are overwhelmed. They are Mary Wollstonecraft nightmares.

You might not agree. You might be an optimist. You think everything is going to be ok. I've heard of those who have gotten through it. I've heard of those pregnant teens that have gone on to college and couldn't have thought of doing anything differently. So-and-so's sister did it—she's a preschool teacher—oh great, reach for the stars. Why don't you become a social worker and make enough money to buy a used car and rent an apartment. Of course there are those that have made it. As Francis Bacon once explained, in a temple hangs a painting of all of those who had said their vows during a shipwreck and were saved—they made it; their lives were saved. Yet, it was asked by the contrarian man, "...where are they painted that were drowned after their vows?" Out of all of the boats that have sunk—how many of those crews have been saved? I bet they all prayed. Just keep treading water—

"Can you allow Maria to go to the bathroom when she needs to— she's pregnant and she's been having some bladder problems," asks the guidance counselor. Maria goes to the bathroom more often than she needs to. God bless her—milk it while you can. You won't have this much freedom for several years—and maybe never again. Even when your mom watches him so you can go out and party late into the night, at some point you will have to go home and hold a crying baby. You will always have to come home and hold a crying baby. Drink up. Stay up all night, your boyfriend just wants to let you how much he loves you, because it's the only way he can truly express the feelings he has for you. Physical sacrifice is good, but embraced in a patch of brown grass near that alley, where it's not as cold as you thought it would be, really means more than anything. He loves you—and the baby has started to bring you closer together. And even though you have to buy formula because he makes you drink with him every night—unless you let him go out with his friends—because your milk smells like a double shot of milky vermouth and tastes like a priests lips—he enjoys your company. You're soul mates and surely will live a joyous life together. Just like the primitives, you have created life.

"—do you have any snacks?" Of course I give her snacks—she's a nice girl.

But, it's not just Maria. It's the girl with the lead in this year's high school play. She has such a beautiful voice. She sings and even the kids that hate everything artful are quiet. Her belly sticks out, and nobody wants to notice. She has such a beautiful voice. It's such a good performance. I'm sure we will all remember her voice. She is creating life.

She will tell her mom she's going to have a baby, and her mom just might secretly be excited because she misses that baby that loved her when she was seventeen years old—those memories have almost died, but she will be a grandmother just in time to make her entire life about taking care of babies and waiting for welfare checks. It's disgusting that you're assuming they are all on welfare!? Make a list and we can have a statistical argument. They have all created life. They have each died a little, but they have created life. They may not be able to take great care of that life, yet they have created it, and it belongs to them.

"You know that's her baby on her notebook?" No, that's not her baby—you're messing with me. That's her sister's baby. That's her aunt's baby. "That's her." The pictures are overlapping, so that's just a pregnant girl with no head. That's not her. "Look that's me." My head is busy with math, as basic as that might sound…you're in 9th grade now, and you weigh about 97lbs, and you have a little girls voice, and you are as sweet as a cupcake, and I think you're a great little student, yet not very academic. You're always friendly and always kind…so you were how old? You must have missed the 8th grade? Wasn't I talking to you in the first place because I was trying to get you to complete your incredibly inadequate response to the writing assignment, so I could initial it and let you leave on time. "I want to have four more kids, but not right now." So, what I'm to understand is that you can barely write a paragraph and you can rarely understand directions, but you intend to continue to mother this baby?

The girls are having babies. Like the primitives they are creating life, and creating death—death of their own childhoods, dreams, and freedoms. Will this death create more life? You are like gods and you are magical, but not because you can create babies.

10

Blythe

I walk into the large corner room. It's 7am, but the sun is already fighting its way through the glass windows near the ceiling. There is nothing in this large room, nothing of character. I sit at my desk, a large industrial office desk. The desks are uniform and new, modern hard plastic slate looking tops with attached metal canister chairs with the traditional hard plastic seats. You don't want to make the kids too comfortable.

As usual, I have no idea what I'm doing. I was too early to seek help from the internet—wireless is science fiction for a few more years, and dial-up is starting to peek out of the woodwork, but content is at a minimum even if you did get hooked in. There is no secret lesson plan you can download. I'm responsible for teaching American Lit. I like American Lit. I even know something about it. I have some favorite writers, but how do I get that information to them in an interesting way that will make them pay attention. And, I don't have 185 days worth of favorite American Lit. authors. This is day one. I can get through day one.

I stand by the door like the more senior teachers told me to. I half greet some of the students as they walk in. "Say, what's up," comes out of a tall black kid. Another man sized white kid walks in with no response. Then, a short pretty girl looks me in the eye, "Hi, Mr. Armendarez. Are you new? We always get new teachers here, every year." "Yeah, I'm new. Welcome to American Literature" I said. They finally all enter and they sort of settle in. I mean, they are acting as though I'm not standing here...talking amongst themselves. Talking too loud at times and saying things that I would not say in front of an adult. Am I an adult? I mean I just graduated from college, and that giant white kid could pass for a 27 year old. I'm 23. I'm standing in front of a class of 45 teenagers. I have no formal training, and the only tips I've gotten were a few days ago from a guy that felt sorry for me, and is retiring at the end of this year. He even gave me his favorite lesson plan. I'm going to save it for a more desperate time.

"Hello, let's see who's here. Ok, keep it down so I can take attendance." I'm shaking a little. I'm sure they notice. The only thing to do is move forward. "Carol Box... is Carol Box here." A hand rises near the front, and it's the kind pretty girl. She sets the tone. Everyone raises their hand rather than calling out, so of course I have to look up and I lose my place every time, so I'm frazzled, even though my finger is planted firmly near the last name I called. So we move forward, and time trickles and breaks off in slow fragments. When I reach the end I see a silent slender girl near the front. "Was Maria your name?" She said, "Yeah, I'm Maria." "Can you take the attendance to the office?" With that Maria became our daily attendance girl.

Palo Verde High School is the home of the Jack Rabbits. In the mid 90's they had one of the highest teen pregnancy rates in the country, probably still do. Not much to do but chase the dragon, run from the cops, and/or ride a dirt bike. You could do your homework, but you're an Indian and ride a bumpy bus home for an hour and a half, or your dad's in the local state prison, which is why you live here and you hate school, or you drive your dad's ford truck to school, and you drive it with pride, your Confederate flag draped over the gun rack, your ambition being to become a taxidermist. You want to open a small office here in town, just off Hobson Street. Do you really need to learn about Romanticism and the canon of dead white poets? I mean they are white and they did love nature, just like you do, but I don't remember any of them projecting a racial agenda or killing things with the intent of stuffing them.

So, it's your first real year teaching and you have a room of American Indians, some Mexicans, some blacks, some whites, a few white supremacists, and some kids of large farm owners and other assorted businesses, all mixed into this one class—what type of results are we going to get? Do you know what you're doing? No, I don't. The only constant is that if you go into the break room before the other teachers you can get a free cup of coffee because nobody will see you didn't place your coins in the honor system cup.

How did I end up here? My brother works at the prison and his wife is pregnant—so my wife who is also pregnant and tired of working her marketing job and cashing the tiny checks I'm getting from subbing decides to look for teaching jobs for me in Blythe. She figured there must not be too many people wanting to teach in Blythe, and she was right. I think we spoke to my brother and his wife twice during our nine month tour of duty. His wife removed herself, reasonably—Blythe is no vacation spot, to the Bay area where her parents lived, to have her baby. My wife followed suit and went back to stay with her parents to prepare for our baby. Blythe had a hospital, but you may not come out alive. I mean no slander. I'm sure they have great people in there. I'm sure they're learning more every day, but they won't be practicing on my wife or my new baby son...I'm familiar with the level of competence a professional new to his field may or may not have.

When our son arrived he slept in a tiny bassinet in our one small room. Once I laid him on the carpet, I knew it might be a bad idea, mainly because the roaches were so comfortable in our small home they didn't wait until the dark of night to come out and join the party. They were domesticated. We had a special set of glasses we used especially for the roaches. We used the cups to cover them, and trap them, when they went for a run across the carpet. You couldn't allow yourself to bother with the ones perched high above us on the cracks near the ceiling, but those that nonchalantly strutted from under the couch into the kitchen to get a snack…they had taken too many liberties.

I laid the baby down, in a mine field of overturned glasses, with handless roaches scratching the smooth glass insides of their prisons with futile swipes. I walked into the kitchen for a snack or a drink of sulfur flavored tap water. I was only gone for a moment. There was a roach, the size of a baby kitten, moving in turtle fashion toward baby's face. I panicked. I was out of cups. With one arm, snack and water in the other, I scooped up baby, and in a nearly perilous motion baby was safely delivered to the couch. I'm not sure how that baby survived its many years with us, but it did.

The kids at school were nice when it came down to it. They knew I was new, twenty three years old, and a little nervous. Even though, I tried hard not to show it. I worked to invent assignments to fill my void in training. Friday was journal writing day—you had to write at least two pages before class ended. I promised not to read them. Johnny likes to drink every day when he gets home from school. Jimmy loves his car and wants to spend all of his extra time racing the oval track out at the fairgrounds. Maria is worried about something, but she hopes it's nothing. Thursday was read about your assigned American Literature time period, in the textbook, and take notes for your eventual lesson to the class on your American Literature time period. Wednesday was a unit on work skills and work related writing that I found in one of the cabinets in the teacher's work room. So really, I just needed to get something together for Monday and Tuesday. Planning wise it was a two day work week, but this job was not about the planning; this job was about crowd control.

"Johnny, take out a piece of paper, stop talking, and sit down!"

"I don't have to sit down; I don't have to do anything. F@@# this Sh@&!"

I was furious. I was too young to be here. Anger welled up in me like a wild dragon needing to devour a village of virgins. I was so mad I could hardly control my speech. My hands and legs and chest began to tremble. Johnny was standing. He played linebacker for the football team. I did not. He weighed 260lbs; I did not. I didn't give a sh@&. I was also an idiot.

"Come on then! Come on then! Come on then, Johnny!!"

The class was at attention. Nobody made a sound. I wish I had something profound to teach them in that moment, because for once they would have all listened, but I didn't. They didn't know what to expect.

"Alright Mr. A" Johnny replied. "Come on then!" I instigated.

Johnny began to walk slowly down the aisle of chairs. At seven yards his eyes were crazy. At five yards they were half nuts, and at three yards they were worried. As he approached me, I could tell he was not going to fight me at the front of the room, so I gave both of us an out, and as he approached I pointed to the door. He silently followed my direction. I followed him outside. The class remained silent.

"You must be out of your F@@^ing mind. If you ever try to challenge me in front of the class again, I'm going beat you're a$$ the next time I see you walking around town. Once I leave this school, it's all self-defense; I'm only a few years older than you. Look how big you are…You can't hide. I see you anywhere else, and I'm going to punch you in the F@@^ing throat until you can't swallow again. You're a big man when you're protected inside this classroom——you're not always going to be in this classroom!"

He didn't have anything to say to that. When a guy who's 5'7" stands in front of you and says things like that—when you're 260lbs with no body fat—you don't know what to make of it. This guy is either crazy, or he really is going to beat your a$$. Even as misdirected as I was, I was lucky he wasn't smarter than me. That might have been my last day as a teacher. I also may have gotten the crap beat out of me.

I never had another problem with him. As time passed the administrators knew I wasn't coming back for another year. I'm not sure they would have wanted me back even if I wanted to stay. I remember the day of my interview, which my wife set up for me. I tried to dress nice, but a sports coat was out of the question—it was over 100 degrees outside and it wasn't even noon yet. This was my first big interview. I went in trying to wipe the sweat off my face. I don't think I stopped sweating the entire time. We sat at a conference table, and the five interviewers fired their questions at me. I felt like I did a good job, but I probably didn't.

As I walked out, my competition walked in, an elderly lady that looked to be crumbling in the heat like a broken paper kite. She was a liability—a health risk. Who do you go with? The kid with absolutely no experience, or the elderly lady that may not make it through the rest of this hot season. Tough choice for sure.

"So, you're in a bucket of rats attached to a rope hanging down a deep dark well, and they are biting you, nibbling your legs away slowly. Your only escape is up a rope that is wet with gasoline, and has just caught fire from the mid-point to a location near the top of the well. What do you do?"

"I would climb the rope" one student suggests. "But, you will die idiot" another students adds. "You should jump out of the bucket" replied Maria. "But the well is dark, and you can't see how far down it is, and how would you get out of the well even if you survived the drop" Joe responds.

"That's a good point Joe" I add. Joe is one of the brightest kids in the town. He wears a coon hat sometimes. I don't know why Maria is wearing a sweatshirt—it's hot like India. You try to walk around the park in the middle of the day, and your body stops working, and you find yourself squatting under a surviving tree branch hoping your entire body won't shut down. Sometimes senseless old people, that are too brave for their own good, get stuck under the shade of the slide—as they wait for evening when they hope the blood flows back from their major organs to their extremities.

"Then just lie down in the bucket and let them eat your face off—what's it matter—there's obviously no way out" Maria replies.

"Let's do another one—now you're the rat, and you're in the bucket. The bottom of the bucket has just been lit on fire. This time a boy is being sentenced for the crime of theft, and his punishment is to be tied down over the bucket. His stomach covers the entire top of the bucket as he is pinned down face first over it. You're the rat. The bucket is on fire. What do you do?"

"This is stupid. You don't have any way out in any of these philosophical situations"—"That's the point" notes some tall bird faced kid.

"I'm just trying to get you to think. What's going to happen without me trying to push you to learn?"

"We don't need you to help us learn! What do you think we did before you got here—you're ridiculous" continues the bird faced boy.

"Ok, let's say we take out the boy and we replace him with a pregnant woman."

"Well, it's her or me! I hope she has a girl—I'm going to eat right through that baby" bird faced boy says. "That's disgusting! You would eat through a baby—that's horrible" demands Maria. "I'm a bucket of rats that are on fire—of course I'm going to eat through a baby!" bird face boy says.

And the highly educational debate continued on. But the bird kid was right. It surprised me a little when he said it. Sure, he's super disrespectful and a little bitch, but he's right they didn't need me at all. The truth is they allowed me to teach once in a while. They didn't learn because I made them, or because I was creative or cool. They learned what they wanted to. I used to watch those great inspirational teacher movies. I would think about how amazing it would be to teach like one of those teachers. The truth of the matter is, it might be enough to just do your best and feel lucky to be a part of moments when students happen to be learning and growing. Blythe is a fish bowl. You can't walk down a dark alley with a 40 ouncer in your hand and stop to take a leak behind a dumpster, without some student walking down that same ally before you've finished.

"Ok, take out your journals—it's Friday; let's do this." "Oh, come on!" a student said. "I like the journal time" says Carol. "Thanks Carol; I'm not sure any other students like it." "Yeah, they do—if they didn't they wouldn't do it." "Yeah, maybe." "You're cool now, but it won't last. I hate those other old teachers. That's how you will be." "I'm not going to just turn un-cool at some point; that's crazy. That's not going to happen." "That happens to all the young teachers. Some of them were never cool, but the ones that start cool never stay cool when they get older—there's nothing you can do about it."

I gave that a lot of thought when I went home and imprisoned roaches in my tiny apartment—in fact I have never stopped thinking about it. Why would I become any less cool? Yet, I guess helping students learn something is much more important than being cool. In fact being cool doesn't seem very important at all. Were your best teachers really that cool? Maybe some of them, but they didn't really need to be, right?

"Hey, Mr. A! Guess what happened to Maria?!" asked Carol. "What happened to Maria?" "You know how she is always wearing a sweatshirt to class?! I thought she was just getting fat, but she was pregnant! She went to take a shower and had the baby in the shower! Right in the shower! Then she came out and put the baby on her bed. Not even her mom knew she was pregnant. She kept it from everyone! So, she called her mom in, and her mom just looked at the baby and looked at Maria—and her face turned red, and she punched Maria right in the face! She knocked Maria out! Maria was unconscious. Somehow Maria and the baby got taken over to the hospital!" "How do you know all of this?" I asked.

"My uncle works at the hospital Mr. A…this is a small town" said Carol. "It's true Mr. A. That's the same story I heard" said Joe.

That was the last I saw of Maria. I often wonder how many of those kids are still around. Years later, when I go back through town, I find myself looking around for my old students. I catch myself looking at high school kids; I have to remind myself not to search through the faces of young kids. Those kids are almost as old as I am.

I remember how excited I was to get out of Blythe. I was in my car driving West on the ten freeway with a giant smile on my face. But, one of my students told me people who grow up in Blythe, even some that live here for a short time, end up coming back at some point. It's funny because I thought that was nonsense when he said it, but I've been back to Blythe over and over again—a Blues festival, a long stop for gas, lunch at the golf course, or for a delicious carne asada burrito at the gas station off the freeway on Lovekin. It never really changes. Sure, sometimes there's a movie theater that's open, and sometimes it's closed down again. There's a Starbucks now, but a drive through downtown with its depressed stores and aged signage brings you right back to your roach infested life, and all of the other great memories and lessons you learned in Blythe.

Daybook Journal: 2/9/99

I walked to the market with my son. He goes super-fast, often I forget that he's with me and I get nervous I'll lose him at some point. I can understand, on some level, how dads forget their babies in the hot car—to return to a roasted child—yet I can't understand a mom doing it. My wife would never lose our son. She made some cookies today; she is always making something for our kids. It seems like that's all she thinks about. These are hard like wood and coal. I might take those to work to see if my students will eat them. Nobody gets hurt when you make a bad batch of cookies. I always have this underlying fear of making one bad choice, or one wrong turn with my kids. Nobody wants to be the lady that forgot she set the baby carrier behind the car when she went back inside to grab something. People have backed right over their babies. Even considering it makes me feel nauseous.

Daybook Journal: 7/11/07

Anabelle fell asleep watching Hanah Montana…now she won't go back to sleep for like ten hours. You're off with your Bunco friends, and Anabelle won't stop talking to me. We did build a snowman last weekend though, right after she got out of the truck, when I had my hands full, but neglected to put the truck in park. It began to roll back. I desperately tried to step on the break, but I kept missing it and hitting the clutch. My whole body was tingling with fear. I thought at any moment I was going to hear a thud as I crushed my daughter with the truck. Finally I found the break. I looked up and over my shoulder, and saw her playing up on the porch. I almost threw up.

11

Spruce Trees and Squirrels

Rocky and Bullwinkle are some funny guys. A squirrel and a moose—you would have to be on drugs to think that up. Nothing but joy comes to mind when you think of those two buddies. When I was a kid I had a paper route, and it was only a block north of the Family Fun Center and Bullwinkle's Restaurant. Every morning I wanted to go there after I finished my route, but my mom always wanted me to come back home. Who doesn't love video games, miniature golf, bumper boats, pizza and a giant Slurpee from the 7/11, right next door?

Five bucks in quarters used to last a long time. If you were a fair video gamer. If you played Dragon's Lair, and were an amateur, your day would be over pretty fast. Yet, if you had mastered the Pac-Man patterns you could be there for half the day. You had to put your time in. It's not like you could go online to find the answers and all the cheats. You had to find a store that just happened to carry a book of that sort, and then read the book. Or, you would have to bully a kid to teach you. Research the old fashioned way. After that you would take this knowledge and you would control the Pac-Man machine for a few hours. Kids would get so tired of waiting their turn they would leave their quarters stacked on top of the machine and go over to the batting cages to kill a half hour.

It was always hot at Bullwinkle's in the summer, and the dirty water splashing up from the bumper boat ride always felt so good. After they remodeled they chased away most of the big kids that came down to bully younger kids out of their quarters. But still, there was always some sense of danger, you always had to watch your back.

Once you hit a certain age, the place lost a little of its magic. It's a lot like the story *Araby*, by James Joyce, where the kid can't wait to get to the bazaar, until he gets there, and it's not as magical as he thought it would be. It's not as mystical and exciting as his imagination invents. With Bullwinkle's the dissolution is less immediate than it was in *Araby*. It just sort of wore off over time. Least of all the fond memories of calling your 7th grade girlfriend, telling her to meet you there with her friends, where sometimes she does, and you become your friend's hero—for an afternoon. That is as long as her friends are presentable and willing to kiss a partially groomed boy behind the fun zone between the urine stains and vomit splotches. Seventh grade was about the time Bullwinkle's magic faded.

I worked near there in college though. I got a job at Spruce Tree Day School. It was a small private school, and I only got the job because I wasn't smart enough to realize I wasn't qualified for it. I walked in one day, said, "Hello, I'm looking for a teaching or subbing job—do you have anything like that available?" They were so nice. An old couple owned the school. They should have told me to get the hell out, but they stood there for a minute—as though they were somehow obligated to find me something to do, or they would be considered rude. "We really don't have anything, but sometimes we need a noon aid"

They asked me about this and that. I told them I had coached and taught swim lessons. Before I knew it I was sort of hired to hand out cookies and drinks at lunch. The truth was I hated kids. I mean not like

I wanted to punch them when nobody was looking, but I'm just not a kid guy. Why would I try to work at a school? I figured it was a private school, with less rigid state credentialing standards, and if they liked me, over time I might be able to teach a class. I wanted to be a high school teacher. Not a little kid teacher—I would rather get punched in the throat than have to hug a little kid, but I needed money. The kids would push a little. They were attention seekers. They wanted to talk to me, and did talk to me. They didn't stop talking until they got those cookies in their mouths. Then, I would collect their tiny cups and napkins and supervise them on the playground. Later, the big kids would come out and I would just stand there and mind my own business. The bigger kids had no interest in talking to me. That was a nice break.

The truth of the matter, which I didn't understand initially, was these were not normal kids. They took a test to get into the school. Their parents were doctors and lawyers. They went on to great high schools and top notch colleges. I was two years from graduating from a state college. Like I said, I talked my way into the job. I ended up learning more from them than they could ever learn from me. After school I hung out with the kids forced to stay after school for a few hours because both of their parents worked and had real jobs with real hours. Some kids would build giant buildings with brick sized blocks, knock them down and start over again. Sometimes two groups would have huge castles erected. They would have to steal or bully more blocks from the other group to add to their tower. Ayn Rand would be proud.

Other kids would play with the plastic kitchen set, usually the girls, but not always. Others would run around. Then stop when I told them to. Then run again. Then stop. Then run… Yet, the kid I learned most from was the piano kid. This kid was here every day. He would play piano the entire time, some sort of classical music. His parents probably told him he had to, but you wouldn't assume that from his passionate key strokes. It created calm. It was the background music of our lives in this one room indoor playground.

Soon, I graduated from being the snack aid and after school guy. I was asked to coach girls' basketball, and boys' flag football. I don't know anything about girls or girls' basketball. I made those girls worse—they probably never played again. In our first game I had our starters in for the first three quarters. We were winning. Then, to be fair, I put in the girls on the bench. But, I put all of them in at once. That didn't go well. By the time I figured out it was a bad idea, it was too late. One of the little girls said, "I told you that was a bad idea," but I wasn't as wise as she was.

The football team was a much better fit. These were the junior high kids. Pretty much every boy in the school played—we had just enough for a team. When I was a kid my junior high team won a city runner up award, so I thought, I can do this. I still had some of the old plays in my head. As it turns out, my plays did help, but one tall kid and small athletic kid were the ones that really made it happen. We rolled teams up. We played one private junior high after another—we were killing it. These were little private schools. But, none of them could have been as small and tiny as Spruce Tree Day.

The day for the championships came. There was no crowd. All their parents were at work. These kids were used to that. They just wanted to win. I wanted to win. Like it always does, it ended up coming down to the last set of downs. We were down by a touchdown. We had to score. I knew we were better than the other team.

We were backed up against our end zone. After this set of downs the game would end. The referee had notified us all. This was going to be it. This was the time to get it done. I went to my playbook. It was two completions for a first down, and we were going to be aggressive. We went five and out on both sides. Yet, it would not be. The quarterback was feeling the pressure of the game, and he overthrew it.

Next, we went with a run play. They would not expect it, with time running out backed up against our end zone; maybe it would loosen us up for a pass play next down. They stuffed it in the backfield. No problem. We only need one big play!

Third down, we go deep post, but this time we dump it off to the week end with loose coverage. He drops it. Damn that kid. Don't ever cry again when nobody wants to throw to you. You're always open for a reason.

Last chance. We go big. We go with our bread and butter, the fifteen yard crisscross pattern. If you can out run the corner, and you can get a fair pass to pull in—you're in the money. We put the tall blond kid on the line. Every kid knew it was coming to him. Stop him if you can! Forth down. Our quarterback drops back. The tall blond kid is wide open. Nice pass, right into his hands. He was headed untouched right into their end zone, untouched! Then out of nowhere his flags fell off. Ok, so what?! He could have had flags all over his body, and nobody could have pulled one. The ball was ruled dead where his flags had fallen off. That was the game. Just like that. It was all over.

It can't be all about the end, as my coach used to tell me, the road travelled—not the destination. Funny, he never gave me that speech after a big win.

It was a tough loss for all of us, yet even though I couldn't close the deal that was not the end of my time at Spruce Tree Day. I was called back a few months later to sub a few classes. I was finally going to get some real teaching experience! I've wanted to be a teacher since I was in the sixth grade. I have, probably to my own detriment, never wanted to be anything else. I dreamed about being up in front of the classroom. Teaching some pearl of wisdom with my students, just as my 6th grade teacher did with the Pythagoras Theorem.

Once the fog of joy dissipated a little, I remembered I didn't know anything about teaching. I barely knew anything about my own major, let alone some sort of 6th grade math or art lesson?

I showed up early wearing my best clothes. Translation: I showed up five minutes early, and I looked ridiculous. I was twenty years old, living with my grandparents, only in college because on paper I was Mexican, so I qualified for EOP admittance. About one percent of EOP applicants end up graduating from college. You wouldn't have chosen me to take your daughter's hand, or walk your dogs while you're on vacation. If these parents would have read my profile, they would have kept their kids home that day. Was I prepared? Of course not. I wanted to do something cool and contemporary. So I brought a copy of Raymond Carver's *Short Cuts*. I had only read a little of it, but I knew it was a "cool" book. At the last minute I made copies of three of the stories.

I walked into the class about a minute after the students had. The teacher had left a lesson. I didn't have any real time to review it, and had no idea there would be a lesson. I just figured I would wing it with my sweet contemporary fiction lesson. I figured they would think I was so cool they would be at full attention. They would hate the thought of the day their regular teacher would come back. About half way through, most of the kids were finishing up, so I thought, "OK, this is where I bring in the cool guy lesson." So, I handed out my copies of *Neighbors*.

So, we begin and it's going fairly well. The stuff is not bouncing off the page, but they're reading, and being cooperative. Then I notice we're coming up on some talk about some guy that "…touched her breasts" and so I use some good teaching, and we artfully skip that after I interject with a reading question. Something like, "What do you think is going to happen next?" Not one student raised their hand and said, "Well I bet the next thing that happens is this dude is going to start touching her breasts." Even if some of them read ahead, like the good readers they were, none of these studious kids would have brought up the breasts.

It went ok, but I wasn't satisfied. I transitioned into the other story to get a fresh start, yet when "He stepped into the panties and fastened the brassiere…[and] put on a burgundy blouse," I figured I didn't have enough teaching experience to walk this tight rope anymore. None of this was going as magically as I had anticipated. After snack break this class would return. I dedicated myself to finding some Carver in here that would knock their little socks off. So, as they came back in I passed out Carver's short poem, *Lemonade*.

It was short enough to get through, and had no complicated twists or turns. "Guys, this poem is about Jim Sears who has just lost his son in an accident." I read aloud, *Jim blames himself*. "Apparently he can't get over the loss." *Jim had to stand and watch as the helicopter grappled with, then lifted, his son's body from the river with tongs.* "Like giant metal tongs you use to turn meat on the barbeque…maybe your dad uses them?" *But God always takes the sweetest ones…* "Sort of pays to be a total jerk, possibly? So, as you can see, he sent his son back to the car to get the thermos of lemonade." *If only he hadn't made lemonade in the first place…*

All of a sudden I hear a little girl making some crying noises. What the hell?! Did someone upset this girl while we were reading? I walk over and ask, "Is everything ok?" "Yes, I'm ok." I walk on. I didn't want to make a scene and embarrass her in front of the class. I continued…*if they hadn't stopped the night before at Safeway…* Then, all of a sudden, a boy comes up and asks if he can go to the bathroom. His eyes are red like he is either on a hard core glue high, or he's also been holding back some monster tears. What the heck is going on? So we read on…*washed and sprayed by some kid who was still living…if there hadn't been any lemons on earth…Jim would still have his son.*

We finish up right about the time the bell rang. This didn't go as well as I had expected. I collect my things and leave a thank you note for the teacher. I hope the kids don't give me a poor report. I take my things and begin to walk toward the front of the school. Before I can escape the owner of the school corners me. I can tell that I'm not going to be able to avoid her.

"Hello, thank you for the opportunity to do some teaching; I really appreciate the chance." She said, "I heard you had some students who were very upset after reading a poem you brought to class. You see, a few weeks ago one of our students was killed in a car accident, and many of our students are having a tough time with it." This has gone even worse than I had thought. "I'm so sorry. If I had known, I would have never had them read a poem with that theme." I stood there waiting for a rebuke. Yet, she was nothing but kind. "That's not your fault. You had no way of knowing what these kids have been through. If you have any problems before you leave for the day, don't hesitate sending them up to talk to the counselor."

As the story goes, one of the Spruce Tree Day School students had been killed in a car accident. He was a good student, a great student in fact, as good and polite as the rest of these incredibly bright and well-mannered kids. He had worked hard, as hard as any of the rest of them. He had earned a 4.0. last quarter. This was not an easy environment to pull "A's" in.

So, his parents took him on a trip to Bullwinkle's for a super fun treat, a valuable and well deserved reward. I'm sure it was a hot day. His parents surely had a plan for hitting the batting cages, bumper boats, and miniature golf. But, as they began their left turn into the parking lot, a car from opposing traffic smashes into them. The boy died.

I don't know if the dad didn't look before turning. I don't even know if the dad was driving. I don't know if the other guy was drunk or sober. I don't know for sure whether they were coming or going. I don't know if the kid was instantly killed or whether he suffered for hours in a hospital bed. I do know that his parents felt the only pain that no one can ever express or show empathy for. I used to think that, objectively, maybe God picked only the best people—only those good enough, only those who were ready. The most evolved of us. What better way to get a glimpse of God's perspective than to lose your son, just as God had? You must be pretty special to have that lesson reserved for you. To be put on that pedestal. But, nobody wants to be that good. That's ridiculous. To come up with a response like that shows how futile our human abilities are in attempts to empathize. There is no appropriate explanation for this experience. That boy is frozen in time for all of us. *And he remembers sweetness, when life was sweet, and sweetly he was given that other lifetime.* We remember basketball games, building block towers, playing in the toy kitchen, making my block building bigger than yours, the kid that played piano, the tiny cups at recess, and the football championship we almost won.

They remember their friend that died, on a magical journey to The Family Fun Center, because he was good.

Daybook Journal: 2/5/2002

I killed a bird today—I was driving to the video store, and as often will happen a big bird was walking in the street. At any second I supposed this bird would fly away, but that was not to be the case. I felt a thud, and saw a clump of feathers float up behind my car in the side mirror. In my rear view I saw the bird in the road. I saw the head, fully attached and functional, the hindquarters and tail feathers completely intact. The middle was smashed down with what appeared to be a tire groove imprinted through the middle of it. The head was bobbing back and forth as though the bird was trying to loosen its middle from the hot gravel. It looked like it was hot glued down, as if the bird believed that if it could lift its flattened middle its tail might follow. I curled my toes, and drove on hoping to never see that bird again. That bird was in the wrong place. It should have never been there. It didn't belong there. It should have been flying through the clouds.

12

Teacher's Aid

Why don't I have you work with Yvonne? She's not working at grade level, and really the work is not as important as her getting a chance to be around kids her age. Work with her for about ten minutes—just go through her schedule and take a look at how she's doing.

Sure coach. I'm not great in math, but I'll do my best to help her.

I reluctantly walk down the hall to her class. It's not what you would call a normal classroom—it's *Romper Room*. Couches, chairs, weird blocks, what I think is a vacuum cleaner, and a set of cubbies.

I'm looking for Yvonne. Is she here?

She's over at the desk.

She sure is. She's in a wheel chair. She's heavy set—sort of sausaged up in the arms and leg areas. She's wearing some very tight spandex type of shirt that encases her arms down to her wrists. She's not attractive. I smile at her; she smiles back eagerly.

Hello Yvonne, my wresting coach asked me to come help you with your work.

She smiles again. I sit down across from her, take her workbook and begin checking some of her math. I know she's not working at grade level, but this looks like grade school stuff—pages with bright colors and little pictures of fire trucks in the corners of the page. It makes me want to transfer out of Geometry and get into this class.

Well, it looks like you made an error on number four, but the rest of these look good.

Ok, those are hard for me—can you show me how to do those.

I take my time, and I speak in a soft voice—like somehow she's going to understand me better if I speak softly. I'm pretty much doing the problem for her, and she's making no sort of comment, or any type of reaction that makes me think she understands any better than she did.

Do you want me to do another one?

No, I think I understand it a little better.

Ok, I'll see you tomorrow Yvonne.

Ok, see you tomorrow.

I knew I wouldn't be at school tomorrow. I only come to school every few days. It's near the end of the year, and I'm eighteen years old. I can sign off my own absences. I can miss a lot of days and pass my ceramics classes, English for retards, T.A. with Yvonne—and maybe even pull a "D" in that stupid Geometry class. Not only that this is my first year at this school. I'm a senior. Who transfers when they're a senior, right? I had some issues—so I transferred. I'm just trying to put my time in so I can move on. It's not a time for lasting friendships.

I walk to the library because that's what I do at lunch. It's a round building, which makes it sort of cool for some reason, and there are kids walking around with both straps of their backpacks up across their shoulders. Most of them wear collared shirts. I have a t-shirt on with some old faded shorts. I want to be them, but don't think I can catch up. I walk around and look for books. If they have gold leaf covers and look classic I pick them up and read a few pages. I read the authors names and try to remember if I've heard their names before. Usually I have no idea. It feels like I'm getting smarter, but I'm not sure I understand most of the words on the pages.

Last year, back at my former school, I thought I might end up being Homecoming King—now I'm sitting by myself in a library reading books. Later this week I will conveniently miss the panoramic senior picture, and next month when the rest of these guys are walking up to get their diplomas, I will be…well, I won't be there. They say graduations are for the family. With my mom in prison, and my grandmother sitting in her chair wheezing through the last stages of emphysema, I don't see a real point. The bell rings. My bookish friends file out, and we are herded back to class. Soon enough I'm back with Yvonne. We carry on with corrections and mini lessons.

Yvonne, you only missed a few of these today. Nice work.

Are you usually busy on the weekends?

It depends—but I'm usually pretty busy.

Is she wanting to ask me on a date? I'm panicking a little in my head. I'm rapidly formulating elaborate excuses. But, she's not following up with another question. She asks if I can check her paragraph structure, and we finish and I start my walk across campus.

When I enter the "Horseshoe"—where the cool seniors hang out—I stand at the edge and look for someone that has an inviting face. I don't know why I'm trying to stand here. I feel completely out of place. I know I look out of place, but something makes me stand here. I can tell none of these people want to invite me in—none of them are going to talk to me. Don't they know that I'm a senior and that I'm cool—well, that I was cool…just a few months ago at my old school? My old school where I had a ton of friends. They were normal kids—we stood in the "cool spot" at our school—where all the cool kids stood. I stand here for a little longer, longer than I need to, longer than I intend, and some kids glance at me, accidently, uncomfortably. I walk away. I know what types of comments they make. "What's up with that guy—seems a little weird. Why does he try to hang out—he doesn't know anyone. He's not one of us; he's just not our kind of person." I won't stand there again—but for some reason I felt like I could stand there because I deserved to stand there after my thirteen years of school. The bell finally rings. My coach, standing in the doorway of his classroom, stops me.

How is Yvonne doing?

She's doing ok, coach. I don't think I'm really helping her, but she's doing fine.

Remember, most of these students don't have a very long life-span. Don't worry too much about helping her. It's just good for her to be around some other students her age that aren't dealing with the same problems she's dealing with.

What kinds of problems does she have?

She has muscular dystrophy, along with a rare bone disease, which is why her arms are a little short, and her legs can't support her when she walks.

For some reason I wake up thinking about Yvonne. It's dark. My room at my grandma's house used to be a junk room my grandfather build himself and attached to the back of the house. It's the size of a large walk-in closet. I own a mattress and a pile of clothes. I could use a positive change, so I decide to go to school today. I can't miss Geometry anymore. My first two hours are spent in ceramics. For some reason I have no skill for making things out of clay. I make a vase and it's no bigger than a mug. If I got stoned every day, like those guys I used to dismiss, smoking and laughing out behind the trees in the park after school, I bet I could make beautiful vases. Those stoners always spin giant vases. Some day they will grow long beards and wear man bags made of hemp. They will meet a girl that wears a sun dress. She picks wild flowers to gently place in one of her boyfriend's giant vases. They will be persuaded, by their girlfriends, to stop eating meat, yet for some reason they will start to read entirely too much philosophy, primarily Nietzsche, and they will become fat. Maybe even too fat to make giant vases—yet they will have already made so many giant vases it will make no difference. They will be happy, surrounded by other bearded friends with assorted hippie girlfriends. They will be surrounded by their people. They will fit in. Yet, they are of no consequence. They are not directly in my world. They are not directly in Yvonne's world. Where are my people?

I sit in ceramics and spin my wheel. I stick my thumbs in the middle of the clay, slowly pushing my thumbs apart as the wheel spins. Behind me the two loud freshmen girls ask a boy if he's heard the joke about the guy stranded on his rooftop during a flood who prays for God to save him. A guy in a rowboat stops by and says "I have room. Jump in." But, the guy says, "No, thanks. God is coming to save me." Then, a motorboat comes by with the same result. Finally, the helicopter guy shows up and says, "Hey, grab the rope. I'm your last chance." Yet, the idiot says, "No, God is coming to save me." He dies, and God says, "What more did you want? I sent you a rowboat, motorboat, and a helicopter." The freshmen girls laugh, and because they are pretty the boy also forces out some laughter. My cylinder begins to form, yet the sides are uneven, too thin and lack any sort of symmetry. Soon the entire cylinder becomes unstable under the speed of the wheel and the entire essence of its shape is distorted and destroyed. I blame the freshmen girls and their stupid joke.

Some students have given up early. A girl bets another girl she can do a pull-up from the door jam. It's one of those tall metal door jams with the window above it. She turns her palms up and jumps in the air to grab the window jam for a chin-up. As she brings her legs up, she shows her whole world to the group of guys standing there to view this miraculous feat of strength. Nobody will remember whether or not she completed the pull-up. I walk away. It just doesn't seem to matter. Very little of this seems to matter. This girl is not in my world. She is not in Yvonne's world.

***

Hey Yvonne, what are you working on today?

I just have a page to read, and then I have to answer some questions. I've done a few already.

Good work [I notice it looks like a guy with a broken hand wrote it] I'll wait while you finish the other ones.

Ok, I'll hurry.

She looks down, and away, but still faces my direction. She slides a small card toward me. It's a slow push. It slides upon its edge in slow motion. She stops pushing it. The small card seems oddly too far from me to reach. She looks up slightly, out of her crooked downward position.

I'm having a party—that's my invitation.

Oh, thanks—that's nice. I'll see if I'm doing anything that weekend.

It's my birthday. We're going to have it at the San Dimas Canyon Park. My dad has it all set up. I hope you can come.

I feel a little bad because as soon as I put Yvonne's invitation in my pocket, I know I'm not going. She's a nice girl, but a little weird, and she's not really my kind of person. I mean I should do it, but that would be one of the longest days of my life. I don't want her liking me too much, or forming some sort of crush. I bet her dad will set up some sort of bounce house for the little kids. He will bring out platters of food, jugs of punch, with tins of cake, maybe yellow cake with sweet icing. For sure there will be streamers, banners, signs with blue, green and yellow color combinations. It's a giant park with tons of people having birthday parties, with park benches and built-in barbecues every thirty yards. Up above the park there's a zoo filled with broken down animals rescued from the nearby foothills, a bear with a wounded arm, a bird that used

141

to fly, and a raccoon family that has lost their home. I'm sure it won't really matter to her if I don't show up.

**

I can't seem to remember anything about the rest of that school year. At some point my coach got word to me that Yvonne had passed away. Years later, when it was too late, I finally realized all those people were in my world. As I stood at the edge of the "Horseshoe" waiting for someone to save me, God sent me a helicopter, and I refused to grab the rope that might have led us to safety.

Daybook Journal: 2/12/1998

It's going to take me forever to give you this journal. I thought I would have filled it by our Anniversary...I wanted to do something special, but you know how I am...a dreamer and not a dream maker. You're right...I have all of these dreams, and they're good dreams— positive dreams...dreams that would be possible with the right measure of effort. But, my dreams are all over the place; maybe that's the problem. I want to buy a house, be a good father, be a better husband, buy a nice car, be a writer—someday publish a book. I can't even remember them all.

Daybook Journal: 1/12/2006

Today, twelve years ago, you rode a bus into town holding our marriage license application that we signed the night before while watching an episode of *Friends*. You got off the bus with your fifty dollar application fee, and we started our life together. The sun just began casting its shadows over the valley, and I was cold, working halfway up the mountain in the ski hut with the guy who took his morning break to smoke some weed. There were a few times that morning I thought I might be able to ski down the mountain right now and drive to city hall—I can stop her…did I really want to be married? Yet, outside the tiny ski hut, my boots crackling with each step over the freshly groomed snow, looking out over the snow covered hills and into the mirror in the sky, breathing in the smell of brisk cold air, the child in my heart did rise above. The seasons of our life have often been difficult to handle, yet always possible with you by my side. I have only one life to give, and only one love. This journal contains ten years of notes and stories of our family, our struggles, and our most cherished moments. Happy Anniversary!!

13

Po'boy

There was a time when my mom used to make my brother and I a Po' boy sandwich just about every day. They were frozen sandwiches she heated up and slathered mustard all over. It was meat, not really ham, or any sort of recognizable beef, stuffed into a hard submarine roll. You would eat it like you were in prison, forearm flat on the table blocking your plate, head hunched low over the plate with only an inch of space between you and your next bite. I'm not even sure why, because there was nobody there to steal our food. I think that's just the way poor people eat. The one thing you know you have is this sandwich, and nobody is going to take it from you. We ate those dripping Po'boys as fast as we could before we went out to play.

I don't know how I was always fat. I don't remember us ever having more than ten cans of food in the cupboard. Of course, how does any poor kid get fat? They eat cans of lard mixed with bags of beans and rice. They eat like they're in a food eating contest, their minds too slow to register at the rate their stomachs are receiving the food. By the time the mind and the body get on the same page it's too late; you're fat. My brother looked like he came from apartment life. He was the skinny kid that always wanted to get bigger and stronger. No matter how many cans of hash and spam he ate he never seemed to gain any weight. He made weights out of furniture and rocks; it never seemed to make much of a difference. Eventually he did turn into the guy on the Weider Bodybuilding System pamphlet, but that was years later. He just wanted to be a big football guy; I just wanted to be the skinny kid.

My mom only took us clothes shopping once a year. We didn't go to a fancy store to buy fancy clothes. We went to Kmart and bought whatever was on sale. Kmart is bad enough, but the sale rack at Kmart is horrifying. There were some years I would ask to buy just one nicer item instead of the normal three pair of pants and four shirts. She thought I was too good for the family. She brought it up every time she got the chance. "Little Dougie always needs to be stylin'—he would rather buy one expensive shirt than three pair of pants, and four shirts!" She said it like I was some sort of fashion criminal, like I had shunned the entire respectable poor community with my actions. I had tried searching for that one spectacular item in the Kmart boys' section. Maybe I was too good for the Kmart sale's rack?

Growing up we wore Trax shoes. Not track shoes. These were shoes called Trax. They were the Kmart shoe. Sure, other kids wore them, but they were also poor bastards. You avoided them because if you were with them—now you are a group of poor bastards. I tried to blend in with the middle class kids, but I'm pretty sure they knew who I was. The worst part of the Trax shoe is they had stripes like they were trying to look like an Adidas or Nike, it was obvious they weren't. You're like a soldier at war who looks down at a picture of his family, knowing it resembles his family, but it's just a piece of paper reminding him of something he doesn't have. He puts his head down and wishes to one day have the real thing.

So, I was sporting the Trax. We also got the Kmart pants. They were like jeans, but they weren't jeans. They came in weird colors, like maroon and crazy blue. They didn't fit like jeans. They didn't fold or bend right. It's like the creases were all in the wrong places. They didn't give very much. They were a rigid starchy polyester blend of confinement.

We did go to a normal middle class school though, which was good and bad. It was good because I wanted so badly not to be the poor kid, but it was bad because the presence of kids that weren't poor made it more obvious that I was poor. I even got on the bus one day after school because all the middle class kids rode the bus. They all lived a few miles north of the school where the newer houses had been built. I usually walked south to the apartment section of the town, where we lived—down by the orange groves, the railroad, and the can factory. So, one day I get on the bus, and kids look at me like, "That kid doesn't ride the bus." It was like a club—they were the bus club. They all had nicer lunch boxes with cool thermoses. I was so excited to be on that bus. I don't even know if I had ever been on a bus before? It was a great adventure. We went slow, made some stops, slowed down and stopped at the railroad tracks—where the bus driver looked down the track, which seemed a little foolish. I remember the driver pulling the bus right up and over part of the track—I thought if a train is coming he is only going to have time to say, "Ok, kids the train is going to smash right into us...I hate you bastards."

So, we get to what felt like one of the last stops, and I got off. I was hoping the bus would weave around town so I could get off closer to home. I was now miles away from home. It was a long walk for a second grader, although it was worth it just to be on the bus for a little while.

***

Even though I was not the most fashionable student, it didn't stop me from liking the girl two desks up in the second row. She was the most beautiful girl I had ever seen. Well, Mary Van Dike from first grade was my dream girl, but she moved away to Washington. This girl was still pretty special. She had brown hair—and I'm speaking now completely as my second grade self when I say I remember her having a curvy body—I think she was also very fluid and well poised on the four-square court. She was all I could think about.

I was at the store with my mom, shopping for cans of hash. I asked her if I could buy some Valentine cards. She said she had already bought me a box of cards. I told her I wanted to get something special. There it was!! A giant cookie shaped like a heart. It was covered with frosting. It said something about love and Valentine's Day. "Mom, can I get that cookie!?" She immediately knew what the deal was. "That's not going to fit in the envelopes I bought you." I talked my mom into buying one larger envelope from the card section. I was all set to be a Valentine hero.

I was pretty excited. This curvy girl was going to be so happy to get my giant heart Valentine. It was so big I had to cut a hole in the bottom middle of the card for the tip of the heart. When I got done the giant cookie heart in the envelope looked like a tall man sleeping in a baby's bed…things were sticking out at both ends.

I got all of my Valentines together the night before. In the morning, I went to find a pair of pants, and I couldn't find any that fit. I only had three pair. I wore the ones that fit yesterday. I only got one pair of pants at Christmas, and was already wearing them a few times a week. I pulled on the rigid Kmart pants. They were so tight my thighs felt hot and constricted. I tugged at the snap (they had no buttons for some reason) and I tried to force it together. The fat of my belly fought my efforts, but finally I was strong enough to get them snapped. When I did I looked down and saw that my pants were a good inch and a half too short. I thought I had just gotten too fat, but I had also grown— seemingly all of the sudden. As I walked to school I tried to take short steps. I figured if I took short steps my pant legs might not ride up quit as far. Maybe nobody would notice how short my pants were.

I quickly taped my paper bag mailbox to the front of my desk, and started to pass out my Valentines, dropping them in each kid's mailbox bag. I stayed close to the desks as I passed them out. I was not going to go out into the wide open of the aisle. If I did some stupid kid would say something about my pants. From time to time kids already called me "Fat Boy." You don't want to add another nickname. That just gets confusing. Maybe I would rather be known as "High Water" than "Fat Boy." I mean you can eventually find new pants. Maybe people will forget about it. When Cindi wasn't looking I tried to place the giant cookie heart in her colorful paper bag mailbox, but it just wouldn't fit! I began to panic. Any moment she was sure to turn around and see me putting this giant awkward cookie in her mailbag. Not only that, I was sort of out in the open. Like I said, you want to keep moving if you don't want some kid yelling some negative comments about your appearance. In my panic, I placed it on her desk. I quickly went back to my seat and sat down. I was sweating. The sweat would be dripping down my thighs if there was any space between these burlap pants and my skin. If Spanx had existed—some stupid kid would have yelled out "Spanx" or "Spanx Boy." Kids are bastards. My hands were shaking. What would she say? What would she do? Would she fall in love with me?

I watched her open it; she looked surprised. She slowly opened the envelope. She giggled a little. Then, she read my card: "From Dougie, BE MY VALENTINE." That's all she needed to know. How could she resist that giant cookie?! She didn't look at me. I tried to get her attention. She didn't even look my way. Did she not know it was from me? I wrote my name as clearly as I could. Surely she is going to say something! I searched my mailbag for the Valentine she gave me. I rifled through; there it was, just a normal sized generic card. I opened it with great anticipation. I carefully thumbed open the card. It just had her name—nothing else, just her name. She took no time at all on this. I put time and effort into mine. I persuaded my mom, searched for and retrieved an adequate envelope, cut extra heart shaped triangle space near the bottom and hump space at the top of the envelope, wrote my name as neatly as possible, placed the cookie without breaking it, and then sealed the envelope.

Shortly thereafter the bell rang for recess. I stayed seated until the last kid got close to the door. I looked over at her desk. I didn't see the cookie. I was hoping she enjoys it. I walked slowly out and onto the playground. I looked from the end of the black top and over to the grass where I usually played touch football at recess, although I couldn't play football with these pants on. That would be a disaster. I walked over to the red brick wall of the school building. I sat down on the concrete with my back against the cold brick. I sat Indian style to conceal my pant legs. My button cut into the fat flesh of my belly. I sat there, where the kids usually are forced to sit when they get in trouble on the playground. I was in trouble. This is the lesson I will build my life around. This was a life unexpected, yet given like a punch in the throat. I didn't see it coming because I lived it and wore it like a pair of ill-fitting pants. I didn't sign up for it, yet until now I had willingly lived it. That moment, burned into my memory, changed my life. I looked out at the playground and watched kids laugh and run and be happy. I knew I would never be this boy again.

Thank you for reading!!

If you enjoyed the book please leave a review.

If you would like to hear about future books, or blog articles, find us at

throatpunchlessons.com.

Join our email list, and link up to our Facebook page. I'm always happy to respond to questions and comments.

Made in the USA
San Bernardino, CA
09 September 2016